Experimental Design and the Analysis of Variance

THE PINE FORGE PRESS SERIES IN RESEARCH METHODS AND STATISTICS

Through its unique modular format, this series offers an unmatched flexibility and coherence for undergraduate methods and statistics teaching. The two "core" volumes, one in methods and one in statistics, address the primary concerns of undergraduate courses, but in less detail than found in existing texts, and are both available in inexpensive, paperback editions. The smaller "satellite" volumes in the series can either supplement these core books, giving instructors the emphasis and coverage best suited for their course and students, or can be used in more advanced, specialized courses.

Investigating the Social World:
The Process and Practice of Research *by Russell K. Schutt*

Social Statistics for a Diverse Society *by Chava Frankfort-Nachmias*

A Guide to Field Research *by Carol A. Bailey*

Designing Surveys: A Guide to Decisions and Procedures
    by Ron Czaya and Johnny Blair

How Sampling Works *by Richard Maisel and Caroline Hodges Persell*

Experimental Design and the Analysis of Variance *by Robert Leik*

Forthcoming

Regression: A Primer *by Paul Allison*
Program Evaluation *by George McCall*

Experimental Design and the Analysis of Variance

Robert K. Leik

University of Minnesota

Pine Forge Press

Thousand Oaks, California • London • New Delhi

For information, address

 Pine Forge Press
A Sage Publications Company
2455 Teller Road
Thousand Oaks, California 91320
E-mail: sales@pfp.sagepub.com

Printed in the United States of America

Library of Congress Cataloging-in-Publication Data

Leik, Robert K.
    Experimental design and the analysis of variance / author, Robert K. Leik.
        p. cm. — (The Pine Forge Press series in research methods and statistics)
    Includes bibliographical references and index.
    ISBN 0-8039-9006-5 (acid-free paper)
        1. Analysis of variance. 2. Social sciences—Statistical methods.
    I. Title. II. Series.
    HA31.35.L44 1997
    519.5'38—dc20   96-35668

This book is printed on acid-free paper that meets Environmental Protection Agency standards for recycled paper

Production Editor:	Sanford Robinson
Designer:	Lisa Devenish Mirski
Cover Design:	Paula Shuhert and Graham Metcalfe
Typesetter:	Janelle LeMaster
Indexer:	Cristina Haley
Print Buyer:	Anna Chin

About the Author

Robert K. Leik is Professor of Sociology and Associate Dean of the Graduate School at the University of Minnesota, Twin Cities. His areas of interest include mathematical sociology, statistics and methods, computer simulation, social psychology, and the family. His current research involves a longitudinal study of Head Start families, the social consequences of structures such as the European Union and the North American Free Trade Agreement, a series of computer simulations of interaction processes, and an analysis of the nature of nonlinear structural models.

About the Publisher

Pine Forge Press is a new educational publisher, dedicated to publishing innovative books and software throughout the social sciences. On this and any other of our publications, we welcome your comments and suggestions.

Please call or write us at

Pine Forge Press
A Sage Publications Company
2455 Teller Road
Thousand Oaks, California 91320
(805) 499-0721
E-mail: sales@pfp.sagepub.com

Visit our new World Wide Web site, your direct link to a multitude of online resources:

http://www.sagepub.com/pineforge

Charlie Brown would no doubt have dedicated a book to his little red-haired girl. In the same spirit of wide-eyed amazement at the wonder of such a special person, I dedicate this book to the redhead in my life: sociologist, experimentalist, and partner for many wonderful years, Sheila A. Leik.

Contents

Series Foreword

The Pine Forge Press Series in Methods and Statistics, consisting of core books in methods and statistics and a series of satellite volumes on specialized topics, allows instructors to create a customized curriculum. The authors of the core volumes are both seasoned researchers and distinguished teachers, and the more specialized texts are written by acknowledged experts in their fields. At present the series offers the core texts in research methods and statistics and satellite volumes focusing on sampling, field methods, survey research, and experimental design and the analysis of variance. Soon to be published are additional satellite volumes on such specific topics as regression analysis and evaluation research.

Robert Leik's *Experimental Design and the Analysis of Variance* offers a rigorous and exceptionally clear development of the principles of designing and analyzing experiments. Assuming only an introductory background in the logic of statistical inference, it starts with elementary principles and treats its subject matter very fully, asking the student to take nothing for granted. Beginning with general principles of experimental design and the statistical concepts needed for evaluating such designs, Professor Leik develops a single example to build from the simplest, (one-way) experimental designs to multifactorial and repeated-measures designs. The step-by-step approach is designed to enhance the student's understanding of the mathematical basis for analysis of variance techniques, the use of SPSS to conduct the analyses, and the substantive context within which they are used and interpreted.

The book is brief enough to be used with the core text by Chava Frankfort-Nachmias, *Social Statistics for a Diverse Society,* to deepen the student's general understanding of statistical analysis and to extend coverage in the introductory course to specific techniques for designing and analyzing experiments. Or it might be combined with selected satellite volumes such as the one on regression. As a concise, yet complete how-to book on experimental methods, this volume may be used in conjunction with a substantive text in courses that employ experiments.

—*Kathleen S. Crittenden*
Series Editor

Preface

This book provides an introduction to designing experiments and to analyzing data using the statistical method called analysis of variance, or ANOVA for short. At first, these may sound like unrelated topics. Experimental design concerns random assignment, control, manipulation, and measurement. Like all statistical procedures, ANOVA concerns how confident one can be about the conclusions reached by statistical tests, hence with questions about sampling methods, data properties and distributions, and theoretical test assumptions. However, all good research design must keep in mind the way in which the data are to be used, and all good statistical analysis depends on the way in which the research was conducted. In the case of experiment design and ANOVA, these two foci work particularly well together. The logic of ANOVA was developed with experimental evidence in mind, and the design of experiments has evolved to be particularly cognizant of the needs of ANOVA for handling the data.

Chapter 1 discusses the essence of experimental design, the idea of causality, criteria for good experiments, controlling error, and internal and external validity. To a considerable degree, these topics are covered in the core methodology text for this series, but they are crucial to understanding experimentation and the analysis of experimental data. Chapter 2 reviews statistical concepts so as to provide a clear understanding of the logic of statistical inference. An actual experimental study is described, and the resulting data are reproduced. The study provides a single common thread throughout the subsequent development of simple to more complex research designs and their accompanying ANOVA models.

The simplest form of ANOVA is introduced in Chapter 3: one-way ANOVA. In this chapter, as in the rest of the book, it is assumed that complete understanding of the statistical method requires understanding the mathematical equations involved as well as the logic. Most statistical calculations these days are accomplished by computers, of course. Yet, good application of statistical methods requires clear understanding of what the "number crunching" involves. Understanding equations, however, does not require a lot of mathematical background. All symbolism used is carefully explained, and each new equation is explained step by step to ensure that the meaning is clear. Throughout the text, after equations are introduced and explained, computer-generated results using SPSS-PC are provided with explanations of the necessary command lines used to run SPSS-PC. The SPSS results consistently are related to calculations previously done using the formulas and data presented. It is recognized that SPSS for Windows is gaining increased popularity, but the differences between it and SPSS-PC are minor. The reader should be able to use the Windows version with ease if the intent of the instructions is understood.

Chapter 4 introduces two concepts not normally encountered in introductory statistics courses: contrasts and effect sizes. The basic one-way ANOVA tests a single null hypothesis that, on the average, all treatment groups in an experiment (or all different populations sampled) do not differ significantly with regard to a specified dependent variable. Rejecting that null hypothesis does not specify where significant observed differences occur. For example, with three treatment groups in an experiment, is a significant ANOVA result due to treatment A being different from treatments B and C whereas the latter two do not differ, or are all three groups different, or is some other pattern present? Contrasts allow designating and testing very specific group comparisons within the larger ANOVA logic. Effect size is a way of referring to how much actual difference a treatment has made. The concept links statistical results with the question of substantive or theoretical importance. An experiment might have a really small effect, but if there are large enough samples in the study, then the effect might be statistically significant (i.e., it probably did not occur by pure chance). By contrast, an experiment might have a very large and theoretically important effect, which may or may not be statistically significant depending on the sample sizes involved.

Chapter 5 moves ANOVA beyond the one-way model to designs that can test more than a single idea in the same experiment. As new equations are introduced, each is presented both in mathematical form and in step-by-step descriptions in the accompanying text. The emphasis throughout is on melding statistical logic with that of designing more complex experiments. A different type of extension of the ANOVA logic appears in Chapter 6: repeated measures ANOVA. A "classical" experiment exposes a given subject to a single treatment and obtains a single dependent variable measurement. An equally important strategy is to expose the same subject to a series of treatments (or possibly to the same treatment a number of times). Here the subject acts as his or her own control, and the statistical model for analyzing the data has to take that control into account. The two experimental models serve different purposes. Each is an important part of a good methodological tool kit.

Finally, Chapter 7 has two parts. The first extends the concepts of experimental design and ANOVA to more complicated models such as balanced versus unbalanced designs, Latin square designs, and analysis of covariance as a way of statistically controlling for between-subject differences that cannot be physically controlled or sampled for in the experiment. The purpose is primarily to acquaint the reader with a broader array of potential designs and their related statistical models than can be covered in an introductory text.

The second part of Chapter 7 discusses different sampling methods and then introduces the notion of statistical power. It concludes with commentary on the differences among statistical significance, theoretical importance, and practical utility. Statistical power is not a new concept, but the tendency in many courses has been to treat it as an afterthought, if at all. Further, most professional journals have not insisted on power estimates when statistical analyses are presented. That fact seems to be changing. Some editors and reviewers now expect that power issues will be addressed and indeed should be if we are to have a fuller understanding of the importance of research results.

Writing an introductory book on a statistical method is not easy. The literature on statistical methods is immense. Many complete texts are very large volumes that still leave some issues untouched. For a smaller companion text such as this, it has been necessary to set aside many of the topics that would have been logical extensions of or more detailed commentaries on the material that is included. No doubt, different readers will have their own "I wish he had said something about . . ." thoughts. Good! Any introduction needs to be followed up with practical application and with further inquiry into more advanced procedures. If this rather brief volume sparks such application and inquiry, then it will have served a noble purpose.

Acknowledgments

As with any such work, there are many people whose work or advice over the years has shaped the final content of this book even if there is no way to trace their influences. Kathleen Crittenden and Richard Campbell deserve particular recognition; their comments on earlier drafts have been very important. Also, much help was received from anonymous reviewers. My thanks to all. If the book serves its purpose well, then their contributions have helped achieve that end.

1 The Basics of Experimental Design

This book is about designing experiments and analyzing data from them using a statistical method known as analysis of variance. Experimental methods are very common in some of the social sciences but are rarely used in other social science fields. Experimentation is not always *the* method or necessarily even a preferred method of research. That depends on the subject and purpose of inquiry. If one's primary concern is to develop and test *causal theories* about social phenomena, however, then careful experimentation offers the most powerful approach. Why that is so should become apparent as we examine the logic of doing experiments.

Analysis of variance, often called ANOVA for short, can be used for analyzing either experimental or nonexperimental data. It is easiest to introduce it in the context of an experiment, however. After all, initial work in ANOVA was developed by Sir Ronald A. Fisher in conjunction with agricultural experiments. As the logic of statistical analysis of experimental data became more advanced, so did the logic of designing experiments to make them optimally informative. To a considerable extent, the methods developed together. Not all researchers are interested in cause, of course, but most experimentalists are and a lot of nonexperimentalists are, as well. Let's look at the idea of cause and the way in which experiments can help sort out causation from other possible explanations of what we observe or study. For a more extensive discussion of the concept of cause in the social sciences, see Hage and Meeker (1988). For further discussion of experimentation, see Meeker and Leik (1994). Classical references include Campbell and Stanley (1963), Cochran and Cox (1957), and Fisher (1935).

About Causal Theories

Our first concern is to decide what we mean by cause. The first sentence of *Social Causality* (Hage & Meeker, 1988) is the question "Why do things happen?" Such a question implies that we think in terms of cause and effect. The *Random House Webster's College Dictionary* (Random House, 1991) gives as the first definition of *cause* "a person that acts or a thing that occurs so as to produce a specific result." Similarly, *Webster's New Universal Unabridged Dictionary* (New World Dictionaries, 1983) defines it as "that which produces an effect or result; that from which anything proceeds, and without which it would not exist" and goes on to quote John Locke: "*Cause* is a substance exerting its power into act, to make a thing begin to be."

The observation "If he hadn't been driving so fast he wouldn't have crashed" implies a direct link between speed and having an accident. The phrase "speed kills," which used to be the rallying cry for reducing highway speed limits, is a shortened version of that implication. It implicitly says that speed *causes* death. However, the logic is a bit problematic if we want to make an absolute statement. If (excessive) speed kills, then every time someone goes too fast a death should result. The highway data simply do not agree with such a proposition. In fact, simplistic causal statements often run into the same problem, and the concept of cause in scientific inquiry has gone through a period of distrust and rejection. Nevertheless, the concept of cause currently is alive and well and very much a part of contemporary social science theory and research. Determining what causes what is the reason for conducting experiments and for much statistical modeling.

We might consider a more elaborate "speed kills" model that says that as speed increases, (a) the ability of the driver to maintain control and respond to unexpected events decreases and (b) the likelihood of mechanical failure increases. Together, these changes imply a higher probability of an accident, with a concomitant increase in the likelihood of a fatality. Note that this new formulation has introduced two new notions: change in a condition rather than its mere presence and probability rather than certainty. It generally is useful to think of cause in terms of change: If we change X, will that produce a change in Y? This conception of cause is Aristotle's *efficient cause* (cf. Bunge, 1979, p. 31). It is difficult to talk about cause in this sense if either X or Y remains constant, although in certain circumstances one might wish to argue that constancy in X *prevents* change in Y.

We can check on intuitive (or more formal) notions of cause by inducing change in a hypothesized cause, X, to see whether a change in effect, Y, results. That is, we can experiment. However, there may be one or more pitfalls with simply wiggling X and saying "aha" if Y subsequently wiggles. That is, conclusions about what causes what often are suspect. The logic of experimental design identifies and helps rule out the various pitfalls to deducing cause. A short bit of fantasy might help.

Problems of Deducing Cause

Consider an alien visiting us with no knowledge of things like electric lights and light switches. All our friend knows is that sometimes lights are on and sometimes they are off. If left alone to work out how to control a light in her room, she might try using incantations, standing on her head, pleading, or even pounding the walls. Perhaps by chance she hits the light switch and the light goes on. Aside from "Wow—look at that," what can she conclude? Perhaps it was pounding on the wall, and so she might try a few more hits, presumably to no avail. Of course, that might have been what turned the light *on* but not what turns it *off*. How can she know?

Perhaps she remembers hitting the switch, and so she tries that again. If she hits it in the same direction as she did the last time, however, nothing will happen. That could discourage the switch hypothesis and send her inquiry elsewhere. On the other hand, by chance or reason, she might try moving the switch the other way and find that the light goes off. Eureka! A few more on-off cycles and our friend is armed with new knowledge. She can control light— maybe.

Leaving the room to go into a dark hallway, she glances about and sees another switch. "Ah! Just move that up and I will have light in the hall." Suppose, however, that no light goes on. What now? Were her earlier results a fluke? We know that if the hall light is hooked to a three-way switch, then this switch might have to move in the opposite direction, but why would she know that? Even without the idea of three-way switches, she could still try the other direction. If the light goes on, she may conclude that the switch hypothesis is still good but that "it depends." On what it depends might not be clear, but at least she has light in the hallway.

As she leaves the building and finds it dark outside, our visitor wants to turn on a light she sees outside the door. "Ah, there is one of those push-up-push-down gadgets. Let's try it." But nothing happens. Up, down, . . . nothing. Is her budding theory in jeopardy? From our vantage point, we can think of several explanations. Perhaps the switch is for another light, and she just did not notice that a different light was going on and off. Perhaps it is the right switch, but the light bulb is burned out or the wiring is bad or the power is off in that circuit or even in the whole neighborhood.

If she continues her quest, she may stumble on the answer, such as having tried the wrong switch. But if that answer is not linked to anything she can think of, such as a burned-out bulb, then she may conclude incorrectly that the switch-light relationship works only indoors or that it was all a bad theory despite early successes. She may still believe in her theory while recognizing its limits at this time, believing that some day she will master the outdoors part of the problem as well. Of course, someone else may turn on a light when our friend is looking elsewhere, which would mean that the light changes without her doing anything at all. Developing adequate causal theories can be such a headache.

The essence of this story is that by manipulating possible causal agents, it might be possible to formulate an increasingly complex "theory" about what causes lights to go on and off. The theory may not always work. Why the theory works or does not work may not be known (i.e., our friend knows nothing technical about electrical currents and wires and filaments), but at least such a budding theory provides a first step. Without manipulation, however, it would have been much more difficult to deduce the connection between switches and lights.

A Second Example

Consider another alien unable to manipulate switches, perhaps because he consists mostly of vapor rather than hard substance (we know a few people like that). The best he can do is float about from one location to another to try to determine what there is in common between those places with lights on and those with lights off. Then perhaps he can work on the causal question.

Of course, there are numerous possible pitfalls in this procedure. If the quest is during the day, then nearly all outside lights will be off, most lights in windowed rooms will be off, and many lights in windowless rooms will be on (but usually only when someone is present). If everyone was very careful about not wasting energy so that only inner rooms with people in them had lights on, then our visitor may easily conclude, "Having humans in inner rooms causes lights to go on. There must be some sort of sensor mechanism. They go out when humans leave." That would also explain why he and the nonhuman animals he observed could not get lights to go on or off: because they are not human. Very conclusive, yet incorrect. Correlational data would have generated a spurious causal conclusion.

If he watches long enough, he may see one or more people moving a switch just before the light changes. Ah—a new hypothesis. He cannot manipulate the switches, but as he floats around he notes the joint frequencies of lights on or off and switches up or down. From our other friend's experience, we know that the resulting cross-classification is not likely to show perfect association. Some switches will be up while the lights are off. Some will be down while the lights are on. Probably a larger proportion will fit the hypothesis than not, but does that imply cause?

Criteria for Good Experiments

Let's turn to a more careful examination of the problems of causal analysis. Many discussions of experiments as vehicles for testing causal hypotheses start with the classical experimental model. Although it has many drawbacks, it can help clarify what good experimentation should be like.

We start with a hypothesis at the individual actor level.

Hypothesis: Students who have practiced translating algebraic equations into English sentences will, on the average, have higher grades in statistics courses than will students who do not have such practice.

My own classroom experience suggests that this is true, but suppose we want to test the hypothesis formally. The classical model specifies that we assemble some experimental subjects and divide them into two groups, which we will label the "experimental" and "control" groups. All subjects will be measured on the dependent variable, Y, a statistics test for this hypothesis. After the initial measurement, only the experimental subjects will be exposed to the experimental stimulus, X, which would be practice sessions in translating equa-

Exhibit 1.1

The Classical Experimental Model

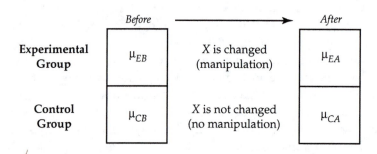

tions into English. Then all subjects will again be measured on the dependent variable, a statistics test comparable to (or, for some research, identical to) the initial one. The important question is whether the two groups differ, on the average, after the experimental manipulation. The classical model is shown in Exhibit 1.1.

Formally, the simplest statement of the statistical hypothesis is that the means of the groups will be different after manipulation, whereas its logical opposite, the null hypothesis, is that the means will not differ after manipulation. Properly, we should be interested in population means rather than simply in sample means, so that the statistical hypothesis will be couched in terms of population means. Remember that μ refers to a population mean. We discuss populations versus samples in more detail shortly. The subscripts indicate which groups and times the means represent: EB indicates the experimental group before the manipulation took place, CA indicates the control group after manipulation (which they did not receive, of course), and so on.

Substantive hypothesis: $\mu_{EA} \neq \mu_{CA}$

Null hypothesis: $\mu_{EA} = \mu_{CA}$

Now there is a possible problem here: The groups might have differed prior to the manipulation and therefore differ afterward even if the manipulation had no effect. A more sophisticated version of the substantive and null hypotheses is in terms of change from before manipulation to after.

Substantive hypothesis: $\quad \mu_{EA} - \mu_{EB} \neq \mu_{CA} - \mu_{CB}$

Null hypothesis: $\quad\quad\quad \mu_{EA} - \mu_{EB} = \mu_{CA} - \mu_{CB}$

Two essential features of experimentation are present in this classical design: *manipulation* and *control*. In principle, these features allow data to address both sides of a causal argument. If Y changes when X does, and if Y does not change when X does not, then X caused the change in Y. The experimental group provides evidence on "when X changes," and the control group provides evidence on "when X does not change." By using the control group, we hope to rule out changes in Y due to things other than X. The ideal results would be that the mean pre and post measurements would be identical for the control group (no manipulation → no change) while being different for the experimental group (manipulation → change).

The idea of control in the classical experimental design is relatively simple: Keep the manipulation from influencing a second group of subjects. That is one form of physical control; the control group never experienced the practice sessions or whatever the causal factor was. It is important to note that there are various ways in which to exert controls in experiments. They all have to do with preventing other factors from intruding on the experiment, but they operate in different ways. Some of these variations will be developed as we look at different experimental models. Similarly, there are various ways in which to manipulate a hypothesized causal factor.

Initially, the classical model said nothing about random assignment of subjects. In fact, it would not have been considered problematic per se that the two groups differed in the pre measurement. The main question was, "Did only the experimentals change?" Because some pre-post shifts could be expected on a purely random basis, however, the more appropriate question was, "Did the experimentals change *more* than the controls?"

There are several reasons why this logic could be faulty. An important one is that if we accidentally had different types of people in the two groups, then perhaps any difference in the amount of change in the experimentals versus that in the controls had to do with factors irrelevant to the hypothesis. It is now widely agreed that a third crucial aspect of experimentation is *random assignment*. Indeed, the view often is expressed that without random assignment

Exhibit 1.2

Three Major Criteria of Good Experiments

Criterion	*Meaning*
Manipulation	Induce a change in the hypothesized cause so as to determine whether the hypothesized consequence occurs.
Control	Prevent other possible causal factors from intruding on and contaminating the experiment.
Random Assignment	Assign subjects to different experimental treatment groups randomly, to minimize the chance of differences prior to the experiment.

one really does not have an experiment (cf. Campbell & Stanley, 1963).

Random assignment does not guarantee that the groups will be alike in advance of any manipulations. Unfortunately, some less careful treatises on research methods imply that it does. What random assignment guarantees is that any differences between the groups will be due to random process, that is, effects that are totally unrelated to the experiment. Therefore, the probability logic underlying the statistical models that we develop will be appropriate for analyzing the experimental data. Any differences between groups should be random if the null hypothesis is true. Our logic will deal with sorting out random versus systematic effects. Exhibit 1.2 summarizes the three major criteria for effective experimentation.

More Complex Patterns of Necessity and Sufficiency

There are several possible causal patterns that cannot be assessed properly with a classical experimental design. A probability logic helps get around one limitation of that design. Earlier notions of cause were deterministic. Change X and Y will change, no probabilities allowed. That notion works only for a causal model that says each cause works alone and works all the time. That is, a change in X is both necessary and sufficient for a change in Y. We now recognize that there may be several causal patterns. A change in X may be necessary but not sufficient, meaning that changing X will change Y

only under the right conditions, such as having a good light bulb and power in the system. The relationship becomes probabilistic unless we understand and control all of those conditions. Alternatively, a change in X may be sufficient but not necessary. In this case, Y may change regardless of whether X does, although it will whenever X does. The three-way switch problem is of this type; the light may go on or off either because the other switch is thrown or because this one is. Again, the overall relationship will be probabilistic unless we know everything there is to know about the system. Finally, X may be neither necessary nor sufficient. This could occur if X is a part of a causal complex that works only if other Xs are favorable, yet that complex is not the only possible source of change in Y. In this case, merely correlational evidence would show little relationship between X and Y even though under the right conditions X may be the crucial trigger that induces change in Y.

Some Other Complex Causal Patterns

More complicated causal notions include thresholds, ceiling effects, interactive effects, developmental effects, and the like. Although we will not go into the statistical procedures needed to assess such patterns, a brief comment on each will aid in understanding why a simple design like the classical experiment often is inadequate.

Threshold effects are such that X will not have an appreciable influence on Y until at least some minimal level of X has occurred. A minimal amount of practice is needed to improve at a sport. It takes at least so much regular exercise to begin reducing the chance of heart problems. If a threshold function is plausible, then it is important that a sufficient range of values of X be tested. One long-standing critique of laboratory experiments has been that, both morally and legally, we cannot create in the lab truly powerful motivators such as fear of death, promise of extraordinary wealth, and the opportunity to take over a country. If some behaviors are activated only by very powerful stimuli, then the ethics of experimentation will never allow us to reach the necessary threshold for the hypothesized causal process. The concept of threshold might also pertain to Y. The idea of a critical mass, both in physics and in social movements, implies that unless there is a sufficient level of Y present, no X will set off changes in Y.

Ceiling effects are just the opposite of thresholds. When a high enough level of a stimulus is reached, increasing it further may have

Exhibit 1.3

Cell Means if Studying and Prior Experience Have Additive Effects

	No Prior Course	Prior Course	
No Studying	40	65	52.5
Studying 10 Hours	70	95	82.5
	55	80	67.5

no further effect on Y. An extra hundred dollars would be meaningless if you already were promised millions for doing the best possible job. The relative increment in stimulus would be zero for all practical purposes. Similarly, at some point Y simply cannot increase further. There is only so much you can do no matter how motivated you are (a point that professors sometimes forget?).

The notion of interaction can be even more complicated. In general, if X_1 and X_2 interact in their effects of Y, then specific combinations of the Xs produce unique effects that are not simply adding up the separate effects of each X. If no interaction is present, then the effects of the Xs are simply additive. A brief illustration might help. Suppose we give a statistics class a short test worth 100 points. Assume that studying 10 hours for that test will raise one's grade 30 points on the average. Assume also that having taken an introductory statistics class previously will raise one's grade an average of 25 points. Finally, assume that if a student did not study and had no prior statistics instruction, then he or she would average 40 points on the test. If the effects of these two conditions are additive, then results will look like those in Exhibit 1.3. The overall means for both rows and columns assume that we have equal numbers of cases in each of the four cells.

Notice that the difference between the two entries in each row is 25 points, the effect of taking a course previously, and that this difference holds for the overall row means. Also, the difference between the two entries in each column is 30 points, the effect of studying, and this difference holds for the overall column means. When both effects are present, their joint effect compared to the

Exhibit 1.4

Cell Means if Studying and Prior Experience Have Interactive Effects

	No Prior Course	Prior Course	
No Studying	40	65	52.5
Studying 10 Hours	80	85	82.5
	60	75	67.5

upper left cell is simply the sum of their separate effects, 25 + 30 = 55 points, hence the term *additive* effects.

Now consider what interaction might look like. Suppose that studying made more difference for students who had no prior statistics training. It helped them catch up, improving their scores by 40 points on the average. Suppose also that those who had a prior course would gain only an average of 20 points from studying 10 hours. As before, those with no studying and no prior course still would average only 40 points and those with only a prior course would average 65 points. Under these conditions, the results would look like those in Exhibit 1.4. Although the top row is unchanged, both cells of the bottom row now are different.

There now is very little effect of prior course experience for those who studied 10 hours. If you check the differences between columns, you will find that they no longer are the same: 25 points versus 5 points for no studying versus studying 10 hours. Neither of these differences equals the overall mean difference of 15 points. Similarly, if you check the differences between rows, you will find a 40-point difference for those with no prior course and only a 20-point difference for those with a prior course, with the overall averages showing a 30-point difference. In general, if there is *no* interaction, then the differences across rows or columns of a table will be the same or very nearly so. If there *is* interaction, the joint effects of the interacting variables will make the differences across rows or columns very dissimilar.

Another way to get a sense of what interaction means is to graph the difference that studying makes for the two groups. Exhibit 1.5

Exhibit 1.5

Graphic Representation of Interaction

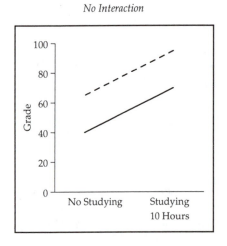
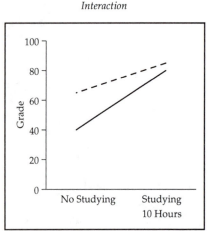

———— No Prior Course group

– – – – · Prior Course group

shows two graphs. The left graph represents the data in Exhibit 1.3, or what things would look like when there is no interaction. Notice that the lines are parallel, which means that the effect of studying is the same for both groups. In the right graph, based on Exhibit 1.4, the lines clearly are not parallel. The gain for those with no prior course has a much steeper slope than does that for the group with a prior course. Nonparallel lines mean that, in this illustration, studying has a differential effect on the two groups, and this is exactly what interaction is all about.

Although interaction sometimes is seen as an inconvenience for interpreting experimental results, it can be a particularly interesting theoretical discovery. Regarding research design, if X_1 and X_2 interact in their effect on Y, then manipulating only X_1 or only X_2 may provide misleading results. Obviously, you cannot design a research project so as to manipulate every possible variable and combination of variables just in case there is interaction in the system you are studying. It is necessary for theory and prior research to provide the clues as to whether you need to design research to capture possible interaction effects.

Perhaps the most problematic causal pattern is a developmental one. The term in used loosely here to refer to changes over time. People, families, work groups, businesses, and all manners of entities change over a life span, and it is reasonable to assume that the changes are at least in part systematic consequences of events and circumstances encountered along the way.

A developmental change in Y set off by some factor X may require a long time lag and the right initial conditions. A great deal of social policy research attempts to deal with questions such as "Does a child's watching too much violence on TV *cause* later violent behaviors?" Such research calls for highly sophisticated longitudinal, repeated-measures designs. They are fraught with great difficulties such as keeping the same set of subjects in the study over a period of several years or even decades without interfering with the causal processes under study.

Exhibit 1.6 recaps the various types of causal relations we have just discussed. In this small volume, we cannot delve into all of the types of research design needed for studying these types of process. Keep in mind, however, that the analysis of cause, and therefore the design of research, is seldom as simple as flicking a switch to see whether the light goes on. At times it is very difficult to hypothesize how the causal process you want to study really works. The best ideas usually are built on prior work in the field, although occasionally a total rethinking of a subject matter may be needed—what is sometimes called a "paradigm change." There may well be times when you feel like our second alien visitor, who can only observe closely and hope to deduce some useful regularities. Remember that a small answer gained from a particular study fits together with other partial answers from other studies, and eventually we begin to understand what we are studying. We do not have to digest the whole complex system in one gulp. The ideal is what Lakatos (1978) has called a research program: a series of experiments (or studies) designed to focus on related aspects of an overall theory.

On Designing Experiments

The ideal is to design experiments so as to minimize various obstacles to getting correct answers. We want to minimize the chance of deducing cause when it is not there while maximizing the chance of deducing it when it is there. If that sounds rather like Type I and Type

Exhibit 1.6

Summary of Types of Causal Process

Type	Characteristics
Necessary and Sufficient	Y will always change if X changes and will never change if X does not.
Necessary but not Sufficient	Y will not change unless X does, but changing X only works under the right conditions
Sufficient but not Necessary	Changing X will change Y, but there are factors other than X which can also change Y.
Neither Necessary nor Sufficient	Changing X under the right conditions can change Y, but other factors can also change Y.
Threshold Effects	a. Changing X will affect Y only if the initial value of X is large enough. b. Changing X will affect Y only if the initial value of Y is large enough.
Ceiling Effects	a. Changing X will affect Y only if the initial value of X is not too large. b. Changing X will affect Y only if the initial value of Y is not too large.
Interactive Effects	A change in X has differential effect on Y depending on the conditions of other variables.
Developmental Effects	A change in X has differential effect on Y depending on when the change occurs, in terms of age, growth, etc.

II errors to you, then good for you. If you do not remember those types from earlier statistics courses, do not worry. They will be reviewed as part of the statistical logic to be developed. Regardless of what you call these errors, stating a causal hypothesis as a statistical hypothesis should automatically raise concerns about the chance of making each type of error.

There are two major approaches to minimizing decision error: manipulating the right factors and controlling everything else that matters. In general, the more our experimental design allows us to attribute variation to known causes because they were manipulated, the smaller will be the proportion of total variation that is treated as error. Intelligently including more manipulated factors in the experimental design does part of the job. The word "intelligently" is used because just throwing extra dimensions into our design may not help and in some cases actually will impair our ability to sort out causal patterns.

As you might recall from a basic statistics or methods course, one way in which to minimize both types of decision error is to minimize the amount of random error in the dependent variable. As always, random error in this context simply refers to observed variation that is not accounted for by any part of the theory or formal model being assessed. Any reduction of extraneous variation reduces random error, hence irrelevant variation in the data. That in turn makes systematic variation more evident. That is, systematic effects will show up stronger against a more stable, less variable background.

Options that aid in reducing random error include using physical controls, using statistical controls, developing more precise measurement techniques, ensuring that the manipulations work, and preventing other aspects of the experiment from biasing the results. Physical controls may derive from the nature of the sample selection, the study site, and equipment. Studying only women will make gender a constant for the sake of the experiment. A laboratory that prevents intrusion of sounds and sights from outside controls those possible sources of extraneous variation. Using computerized or videotaped stimuli prevents accidental variation in those stimuli, again preventing extraneous variation in the dependent variable. The careful training of experimental staff helps avoid accidental intrusion of irrelevant variation.

The important point about exerting sampling or physical controls is that what is being held constant should be a possible source of change in the dependent variable(s) while being irrelevant for the hypothesized cause being studied. To control something that has no plausible effect on the dependent variable is a waste of time, effort, and research funds. It also limits generalization of results to the actual samples or conditions studied. Unless there is good reason to exert such controls, they should be avoided.

Using statistical controls amounts to adjusting observed results to take account of some alternative source of variation in the dependent variable. That allows looking at the results of the manipulations as if the other cause(s) did not operate. For example, it is possible that the effects of having previously taken a statistics class and of studying 10 hours are different for students with a good math background than they are for those with a weak math background. Rather than sampling only for good or weak backgrounds in math, we might ask a set of questions to determine each student's math level. Then we could analyze our experimental results, taking account of the actual differences in math background. In the process, we could determine whether math background explained some of the variation in the dependent variable and whether that effect differed under the different conditions of the manipulated variables. As with physically controlling other variables, however, using statistical controls for variables totally unrelated to the processes under investigation is wasteful and may be detrimental to our ability to sort out what is really going on.

Deciding what needs to be manipulated or controlled, either physically or statistically, is a theoretical problem. Deciding how to manipulate or to effect controls is a methodological problem. Determining whether our results confirm or disconfirm our theory is a statistical problem. Effective design of experiments, then, involves using a combination of substantive and statistical theory in conjunction with sound methodology. Substantive theory says what factors should be manipulated and what other variables need to be measured for subsequent statistical control. Sound experimental methodology says how to do the manipulating and measuring that are needed in the most effective way. Statistical theory says how to do statistical controls, what sample sizes will be needed to be confident in our results, and what assumptions we have to justify to make statistical inferences from the data.

The end product of a good experiment is a set of data, and the conclusions therefrom that we can state with considerable confidence represent the reality under investigation. That is the same as saying that our experiment is valid, that is, gets at what we want to get at. There are two main classes of validity: internal and external. Next we look at possible threats to each type of validity as a way of further considering what good experiments should be like.

Threats to Internal Validity

The idea of internal validity is that the procedures have worked correctly and the measurement adequately represents what we want to measure. There are several threats to internal validity. They include (a) subjects' reactivity to treatments, (b) subjects' reactivity to measurement, (c) biases in subjects' responses generated by inappropriate experimental procedure, (d) biases in the recording of those responses due to observer/recorder biases, (e) failure of a manipulation to "take," and (f) the intrusion of factors external to the theory being tested.

Reactivity to treatment means that some aspect of treatment other than that which was intended has altered subject response. Called the Hawthorne effect, such reactivity was first realized when employees of a Western Electric production unit, who were being observed but not experimented on, increased productivity simply because of the attention they were getting. What had changed in their environment was an apparent interest in their work, although the efficiency study under way at the time had no intention of creating such an effect.

In medicine, the equivalent problem is the placebo effect. If one group knows it is receiving something that is supposed to help, then its members are likely to report feeling better regardless of actual improvement. The standard way of avoiding the problem is to randomly assign subjects to either a treatment or a control group, without telling subjects which group they are in, and then administer an inactive treatment to the controls and an active treatment to the experimentals. In that way, there is no difference between the groups in the subjects' assumptions, and so there can be no confounding effect.

Experimenter bias can occur in many ways. If the experimenter interacts with the subjects in any way, then it is possible by unintended differences in expression, posture, or tone of voice to convey to one group that something more is expected from its subjects. This type of bias has been subsumed under the broader heading of "demand characteristics" of the study. Any factor extraneous to the theory being tested that leads, however inadvertently, to a subject responding to it alters responses from what they would have been if that factor were not present.

At the least, such irrelevant responses increase what appears to be random error. At the worst, should the demand characteristic be linked to one of the experimental design factors, results that appear to support the theory may be a consequence of the demand characteristic instead. Much has been written in recent years about teacher biases and school facility differences that foster achievement in the "right" type of student while discouraging it in the "wrong" type. Because the right students succeed more often than the others seems to validate a social expectation that they are inherently more capable. The notion of demand characteristics should convince one of the spuriousness of such results and the need to avoid demand characteristics in the design of research.

Experimenter bias can be controlled in various ways. If personal contact with subjects by a staff member is necessary, especially during the conduct of the experiment, then it is best if that staff member does not know what treatment is being administered. A nurse administering placebos versus actual drugs could simply be handed the correct treatment for each subject without knowing which it was. Similarly, if a person (rather than automatic equipment) is observing and recording results, then it may be important for that person to be ignorant of the particular treatment each case experienced. Even with the best intentions, a person convinced that a new drug will help alleviate a serious problem will tend to see better results when it is administered. An experiment in which neither subject nor experimenter knows what treatment is being administered is called a double blind experiment.

That form of control is not always possible, of course, but other methods of controlling experimenter bias exist. For example, one can use standardized, impersonal stimuli and automated recording such as via video or computer equipment. As multimedia capabilities increase, we should expect to find increasingly effective ways in which to prevent any form of demand characteristic from operating.

There is another aspect of experimenter bias that is not a demand characteristic: unintentional errors in observation and recording that favor the hypothesis under investigation. Even if the stimulus procedures meticulously avoid any biases, human observers who expect to see a particular pattern of results are likely to see evidence of that pattern whether the pattern exists or not. Perception is not veridical but rather tends to follow expectations, however unconscious or subliminal they might be.

As noted earlier, computerized experimentation allows many types of data to be recorded automatically without going through human observers and transferred just as automatically to machine-readable files for subsequent analysis. Videotaping, especially of multiple-person subject groups, allows capturing objectively both auditory and visual dimensions needed for analysis. However, as yet those sounds and images still need to be coded by humans to be useful for explicit hypothesis testing. Careful training of and periodic checks on coders can help minimize any bias in these stages of the research process.

Reactivity to the measurement process itself is one of the chief problems with the classical experimental design. Your interest in a topic may be dormant until someone asks you questions about it. Afterward, you think about it, notice things in the news about it, and otherwise are altered just because you were asked those questions in the first place. Regardless of experimental manipulations, your "after" measurement is not simply a repetition of the "before" measurement. If that reactivity interacts with the experimental manipulation, then results can be very misleading.

One possible solution to this problem was proposed by Solomon (1949) as a four group design. All four groups would be given a posttest but differed as follows: (a) no pretest, control; (b) no pretest, experimental; (c) pretest, control; and (d) pretest, experimental. Although it was demonstrated that comparisons among these four treatments allow testing the main hypothesis while controlling test-retest reactivity, the design very seldom is used. A large part of the reason may be that the additional two groups double the cost. Experimenters unconcerned with test reactivity see no reason to stand the added cost.

If measurement is unobtrusive or otherwise nonreactive, then there is no need for this more complex design. The best way in which to control test reactivity is to devise experiments that avoid the problem. For example, the way in which children play some games provides direct evidence of factors such as motivation, fear, or desire for acceptance. There is no need to test in the usual manner. If such nonobtrusive or nonreactive procedures cannot be used, then it is necessary to do preliminary research on the nature and duration of the reactivity so as to prevent it from confounding the study.

Another important threat to the internal validity of an experiment is the possibility that the manipulation will not be effective. Suppose that a subject is color-blind and cannot distinguish the difference between red and green stimuli. Or, perhaps a subject is too wealthy to be bothered with a modest economic incentive intended as an experimental manipulation. A more subtle problem might be that subjects differ in their understanding of the language or context in which manipulations were attempted, resulting in differential effectiveness of the manipulation. If a manipulation does not take, then subjects exposed to supposedly different treatments would perceive essentially the same level of X. In effect, X would be constant from treatment to treatment. If that were not realized by the experimenter, then a lack of change in Y would be interpreted as evidence against the theory when in fact the experiment was not testing the theory at all.

Some experimental manipulations are inherently effective. Studies of power in exchange networks, for example, often allow only certain pairs of subjects in a network to be in contact. Computer systems linking subjects in different rooms now are common vehicles both for controlling access by program and for standardizing stimuli and recording responses. There is no way in which the manipulation cannot work; access is the theoretical concept, and access is physically controlled.

When the stimulus is not automatically effective, then it is typical for the experimenter to use postexperimental questionnaires or interviews to inquire about how the stimulus was perceived. There are important considerations for such assessments. First, the subject should be asked any validating questions prior to being told anything about the intent of the experiment. If a subject knows what you were hoping he or she would experience, then a social desirability bias is likely to alter how the subject answers your questions. Second, any such questions need to be carefully worded and pretested so that they do not "tip your hand" about what you were trying to establish with the manipulation. It is too easy to ask leading or inappropriately informing questions. A check on the validity of your manipulations needs to be valid in its own right.

Finally, the internal validity of the experiment may be compromised by the intrusion of a variety of other factors not relevant to the theory being tested. Experiments on families conducted in the families' own homes, for example, are subject to numerous distractions. Field experiments may be compromised by changes in circumstances external to the study such as replacement of key company personnel during an experiment on cultural sensitivity training.

As a particularly bad example of extraneous interference with experimentation, a small group experimental laboratory once was installed in an existing, small, poorly constructed building left over from World War II. When that university's physical plant manager decided to dig a utilities tunnel, having to blast occasionally to remove bedrock, it of course dug the tunnel directly beneath the lab. Periodic muffled explosions and shaking of the building were so disruptive that any study was necessarily seriously compromised.

Exhibit 1.7

Threats to the Internal Validity of Experiments

1. Subject reactivity
   a. To treatment
      Subject expectations about an experiment can influence responses in ways irrelevant to the study.
   b. To measurement
      The measurement process, and especially successive assessments, can create their own effects, either independent of or interdependent with the effects under study.

2. Bias
   a. Demand characteristics
      Behavior or demeanor of the experimental staff and aspects of the setting can induce subject responses that are misleading.
   b. Observation and recording
      Knowledge of expected outcomes can induce unintended biases in observing behavior and in recording both subjective and objective data about that behavior.

3. Failure of manipulation
   The methods used to create variation in one or more design factors of the experiment may fail.

4. Intrusion of extraneous factors
   Factors external to the experiment may intrude so as to interfere with the normal processes under study and confound the connection between manipulations and results.

People just do not go on attending to an experiment under such circumstances.

A well-constructed and equipped laboratory can prevent many such intrusions: noise, confusion, and temperature or lighting changes. However, some extraneous factors can intrude into the best facility because they are brought in unintentionally by the subjects themselves. Prior acquaintance among subjects could compromise a study of group formation processes. Differential external status or expertise among subjects could confound how they behave in an experiment on leadership or social power. People do not automatically tell experimenters all about themselves. For such critical aspects of a study, you have to ask.

Exhibit 1.7 summarizes internal validity threats. All of these threats are concerned with whether the experiment manipulated what it was supposed to manipulate and did not allow any other factors to influence the data.

Threats to External Validity

A common complaint about laboratory experiments is that they are too removed from "real life" to be useful. The laboratory seems artificial, the stimuli cannot be as extreme as they are in the "outside world," and the richness of detail is carefully removed to highlight the specific factors under study. All this amounts to challenging the external validity of experiments. Do they represent anything applicable to life outside the laboratory?

One major concern of external validity is whether the manipulations and measurements reasonably represent what the theory is talking about. This is a standard validity problem for any type of research. Regardless of whether the study hangs together internally, are we studying what we think we are? If I think I have manipulated style of leadership but my subjects see only variations in personality, then I will make inappropriate causal attributions if subject behavior did in fact change. This would be a case not of a manipulation failing but rather of manipulating something other than what was intended.

As to invalid measurement, suppose in my study of leadership style that I use as an index of subject dissatisfaction the number of negative comments made during the experiment. For some populations that would be fine, but obviously it could be very misleading for several entire cultures in which it is extremely impolite to make such remarks. There is a vast literature on such validity problems, so we need not discuss them further here.

A second concern of external validity is whether the controls of the experiment have removed crucial aspects of reality. That is a more difficult problem. Studies of power in social networks typically establish who can contact whom in the network for the entire experiment. The concept of power is one's ability to bargain effectively within the existing structure and how that is altered by structural position (see, e.g., Cook, Gillmore, & Yamagishi, 1983; Markovsky, Willer, & Patton, 1988). Extensive experimentation in this area has provided powerful evidence that network position has a major impact on social power so conceived. However, if the real power brokers "out there" rather than in the laboratory succeed primarily by manipulating who they deal with rather than by restricting themselves to bargaining within status quo linkages, then the experiments do not speak to the real dimensions of power (see Leik, 1992).

It would be inappropriate to dismiss experimentation because of this validity concern. The complexity of the so-called real world often is so great that we cannot tell what causes what. Insightful observation generates initial hunches about how things work, but it takes experimentation to be sure that our hunches are correct. The only real test of causality is experimentation. We may have to be satisfied with small increments in our knowledge of how things work because we can study only very restricted portions of the total problem at any one time via experiments.

That is where the importance of research programs comes in (see Berger & Zelditch, 1993; Wagner & Berger, 1993). Each separate study contributes to a better understanding of a whole too complex to incorporate fully into any one project. The reality aspect of external validity is not best addressed by expanding each experiment to be ever closer to the real world; that would simply make causal deductions from our data increasingly difficult. The most productive approach is to design each experiment to check out part of a larger picture.

One final aspect of external validity for laboratory experiments is the artificiality of the setting. The very strength of the laboratory is at times its major weakness: an environment that subjects can find strange and uncomfortable. If that affects their behavior, then the experiment may not represent how the people actually behave except in strange places. A study many years ago by O'Rourke (1963) had the same three-person families engage in a problem-solving experiment in their homes and also in a laboratory. The extent to which each family member adhered to typical age-gender roles was far greater in the laboratory than it was in their homes. As a study of adaptation to unfamiliar surroundings, the study was entirely valid. If only the laboratory had been used, then any conclusions about in-home behavior would have been quite invalid.

The solution is in being particularly careful about the generalizations made on the basis of laboratory evidence. There is a concept called "scope conditions" that is relevant here. Any theory should contain statements about the conditions under which it is assumed to operate. If there is reason to believe that the particular experimental situation is critical to the effects derived, then the features of that situation constitute scope conditions for the hypotheses that were tested. By being attentive to scope conditions, we not only prevent invalid generalization but we also lay the foundation for studies that

Exhibit 1.8

Threats to the External Validity of Experiments

1. Invalid manipulation
   What is actually manipulated as the subjects see it may not be what the theory says is the causal factor.

2. Invalid measurement
   Indicators of abstract concepts from the theory may not in fact represent those concepts adequately.

3. Controlling out reality
   Crucial aspects of the process that the theory is intended to address may be held constant for the sake of control, and so results may not apply when those aspects are present.

4. Artificiality of the setting
   Strangeness of a laboratory may cause systematic or random changes in behaviors, obscuring the process under study.

---

systematically broaden the scope of the theory. Exhibit 1.8 summarizes threats to the external validity of experiments.

Quasi-Experiments

It is not always possible to satisfy the three principal criteria of good experimentation: manipulation, control, and random assignment. There are several reasons for that fact, a few of which are considered briefly. The term *quasi-experiment* often is used to refer to research that attempts an experimental format but cannot fully satisfy the criteria.

Field Experiments

One type of research that seldom can satisfy all three criteria is field experimentation. That term refers to trying an experiment "out there" in an existing social setting rather than in a laboratory. Examples of field experiments include (a) the message diffusion experiments carried out during World War II, (b) the income maintenance experiments conducted by the federal government during the 1960s, and (c) the variety of attempts in recent years to link work incentives to the welfare payment structure. Actually, there are numerous field experiments going on more or less all the time. Employers experiment with different work settings or personnel policies, teachers try new technologies or other instructional enhancement methods, and universities attempt to create more welcoming conditions for minority scholars. Any time an individual or organization attempts to alter an outcome by manipulating conditions presumed to be affecting that outcome, the individual or organization is doing a field experiment.

There are some clear advantages of doing field experiments, but there are also problems. The major advantage has to do with studying a social phenomenon in its natural setting rather than in the artificiality of the laboratory. Real groups, for example, have histories, group-specific norms, existing status structures, variable resources, members with divergent skills, motivations and distractions, and so forth (see Weick's [1971] intriguing commentary on the family as a group).

When an ad hoc group is studied in a laboratory, all of those factors are held constant for the sake of concentrating on a particular piece of a larger theoretical puzzle. It is very difficult to sort out the relationship between social power and differential access to others in a social network if all sorts of other factors are muddying the research waters. Therefore, much network power research controls such factors via powerful but highly stylized laboratory experiments (cf. Cook, 1987; Markovsky et al., 1988). The artificiality makes some questions unanswerable in the laboratory but greatly enhances the likelihood of answering other questions. The advantage of the laboratory is that we can be much more certain of the direct connection between what was manipulated and what resulted. That is, the internal validity of an experiment is very high when control and random assignment accompany manipulation.

A field experiment, on the other hand, is much more closely tied to ongoing social reality. Consequently, it is more likely to satisfy criteria of external validity. The problems arise from the threats to internal validity: Can we really deduce that the change in Y was brought about by the change in X that we initiated?

Consider a hypothetical study of alternative methods of teaching statistics. Professor Statts has two introductory statistics classes during the same term, and so she uses one instructional method in her 8:30 a.m. class and a different one in her 2:00 p.m. class. The same exams are used in both classes, and at the end of the quarter she finds a modest but significant difference in average performance between the two. Now the problem: Is this difference due to teaching method? Without going into great detail, let's consider what other factors might be operating to create a difference in the groups' performances. To do so, think in terms of the three basic criteria: manipulation, control, and random assignment.

Did something get manipulated? Yes, the instructional methods were different. Did that manipulation take? That is, from the students' viewpoint, was there a difference? Some types of difference may seem obvious, such as giving one class computer-based exercises and not doing so with students in the other class. But unless someone asks systematically whether those who had the computer opportunity actually did the exercises and whether those who supposedly did not have that opportunity did not do computer exercises on their own, we do not know whether the manipulation was successful. In the worst scenario (from the viewpoint of internal validity), if most of the students in the no-exercise class had close friends in the exercise class, and if friends studied together, then there would be virtually no effective difference in treatment. Any performance difference would have to be attributed to something other than instructional method.

Were other factors controlled? Some were, such as having the same instructor and the same overall content of the course. Other potentially important factors differed between the classes: different time of day, probably different classroom, and undoubtedly different class size, to name a few obvious candidates. Time of day is relevant to the professor's and students' energy levels. Differences in setting and class size can have considerable impact on instructional success. If you think about your own classes for a while, you undoubtedly will come up with other factors that could affect this attempted experiment. The important point is that field experiments often take place in settings and under circumstances that simply do not allow for control of other possible sources of change in the dependent variable(s). Without such controls, it is difficult to have confidence that observed results are due to manipulations rather than to uncontrolled and typically unmeasured factors.

Finally, was there random assignment? If registration for Statts's classes took place as it does in most universities, then the answer is clearly no. This is perhaps the greatest threat to internal validity. A moment's reflection will suggest a number of reasons why you might expect students enrolled in the two classes to be somewhat different on the average. First, students tend to end up in particular classes as a consequence of what other classes they are taking and how they can fit an overall schedule together. Suppose the class were offered by the sociology department, for example, but open to others as well. We might well find that because of some other important sociology class taking place at 2:00 p.m., Statts's morning class is predominantly sociology students and her afternoon class is predominantly other students. We know that different majors attract different types of skills and backgrounds. Even if there were no difference in teaching method, we might well expect different results because the two classes do not represent comparable samples of students.

No doubt, there would be other systematic biases via self-selection into the two classes such as those who are morning people versus those who are night people. Without random assignment, this particular field experiment is on shaky ground regarding a logical argument linking teaching methods to performance.

Why Bother With Quasi-Experiments?

You should realize that even laboratory studies may fall short of satisfying the three criteria of internally valid experiments. Many studies of group process have simply imported already existing groups into the lab, such as families or committees. As noted previously, existing groups have important properties that cannot be ignored when theorizing about how groups operate. Yet using existing groups rules out random assignment, and we are left with the question of whether observed effects should be attributed to some manipulation or to group member composition.

In essence, an experiment occurs whenever someone manipulates something and checks on the consequences. When causal inference is at stake, however, internal validity becomes crucial. All this is not to say that a field experiment cannot approach very closely the ideal of manipulation, control, and random assignment. However, achieving this ideal set of conditions in field settings is very difficult and often totally impossible.

Quasi-experiments, especially field experiments, should not be thought of as some sort of poor relative of laboratory experiments. What is gained in the field is reality; what is lost is logical closure. Each type of research contributes an important part of an overall understanding of how things really work. If we have strong evidence of a particular causal process from our lab work, then the next logical step is trying it "out there" to see whether any sizable portion of buzzing reality will be subject to our manipulations. If we have strong hunches from fieldwork but not sufficient confidence that we understand the underlying causal process, then a well-designed laboratory experiment is in order. The two are complementary approaches to understanding the reality we wish to study.

Summary

This chapter has been long and has covered a very wide range of subject matter, from the logic of causal analysis to the various ways in which to design experiments. The two fit together, of course, because the purpose of experimenting is to test causal ideas. As you begin to do research and to analyze the data, keep in mind that the best work is that which forges a strong link between the theory that drives your inquiry, the methods for gathering data, and the procedures for analyzing them. Theory and methods typically are taught as separate spheres. In good science, they are inseparable partners.

2 An Example and Some Basic Statistical Ideas

Chapter 1 discussed experimental design and indicated that the most common statistical method for analyzing data is analysis of variance, or ANOVA. Rather than plunging into a formal discussion of ANOVA, however, it will help to set the stage by a short description of a relatively simple experiment. Then we can review a number of statistical concepts that probably are familiar to you so that the logic and computations in ANOVA will be easier to understand.

The experiment described in the following was done many years ago and is not presented as the perfect example of how to do experiments. Instead, what was done presents a basis for pinpointing critical issues in experimental design and how data analysis accommodates those issues. Actual data from the experiment will highlight the problem of statistical inference that ANOVA is designed to resolve. Expanding on the ideas of that experiment will lead naturally into expansions of both logics: designing experiments and conducting ANOVAs.

The Experiment

Many years ago, a few of us were sitting in a small group laboratory discussing our current experiments on aspects of interpersonal influence in groups. As is common in many experiments, we had been using a confederate, that is, a member of the research staff who appeared to be just another experimental subject but was trained to act in one of a set of standardized roles during problem-solving group discussions. For convenience, we will refer to the confederate as a *stooge*, a term that commonly has been used to mean a confederate whose role in the experiment is unknown to the other participants. This usage is in no way disparaging of the person acting that role.

The experiments were designed to test theoretical propositions about how specific differences in behavior of one group member could affect the way in which the group functioned. Both the basic hypotheses of the study and the experimental methods were derived from prior work by other researchers and ourselves. That day, however, our stooge[1] had arrived dressed quite differently from her usual attire. After the lab session, we started speculating on whether the difference in her style of dress could have affected the others' perceptions and evaluations of her behavior. If so, then her appearance could have resulted in effects that had nothing to do with the hypotheses we were testing, effects that would look like random error in terms of those hypotheses but might in fact produce systematic errors in our conclusions.

The use of stooges had been fairly routine as an experimental technique for years. However, we realized that there had been remarkably little research done on the effects of uncontrolled and unmeasured aspects of stooges such as physical appearance, clothing, and demeanor other than that dictated by the stimulus role. Of course, appearance and demeanor can influence person perception in areas such as attractiveness and personality, but could they also influence evaluations of presumably objective aspects of stooges' behavior? Were aspects that routinely had been considered irrelevant to an experiment in fact altering results? Although research hypotheses usually are derived from existing theory and research, we realized that there was a new question to be explored before we could trust our other research.

We soon were planning a new set of experiments to answer that question. For example, would the content of group contributions from an attractive, well-dressed stooge be evaluated more highly than that from a plain bookish stooge such as a stereotypic "schoolmarm"? (Well, it *was* quite a few years ago.) Again, would the objective contributions of a stooge who acted very confident in his or her role be evaluated more positively than those of someone who was more hesitant, even if the objective contributions of the two performances were identical?

Two problems arose. First, if we were to prevent contamination from yet other aspects of the stooge, then we really would need one person to play both types of role or to present both types of appearance. Could anyone be that different on demand? Our stooge said

"Wait a few minutes" and left the lab. When she returned, we were amazed at how dramatically she had changed. She could indeed look like either a classic "pretty coed" or a drab drudge, and her background in drama ensured that she could be effective in playing either role.

The second problem was to find a task that could allow highly standardized content of the stooge's objective contributions in a problem-solving context while allowing for behavioral variations in how those contributions were made. Again, our star of the day made the most useful suggestion: adopt the well-known *20 Questions* game. Over several weeks, we gradually evolved necessary procedures for a sound experiment on unintended stooge effects. During that time, our original stooge finished her degree work and left the lab. The results presented in the following used a different stooge, but the procedure owes much to the suggestions of our original star performer. The following, then, describes one typical session of the experiments we eventually ran[2] (see Leik, 1965a).

Procedure

Four subjects were brought into the lab. Three were naive subjects and one was the stooge. All subjects were undergraduate students at the time. The lab was arranged with a table and chair in one corner, facing the center of the room. Across the room, facing the first table, were a long table with three chairs and a game master's table and chair. One subject, the game player, sat at the lone table while the others, the observer/raters, sat at the long table. Exhibit 2.1 shows the basic arrangement of the laboratory.

Everyone was told that, one at a time, they were going to play *20 Questions*. That is a game in which players try to guess what object the game master has in mind by asking a series of yes/no questions. At the outset of each game, the game master simply states whether the object to be guessed is animal, vegetable, or mineral. Typically, anything real or imaginary, anything living or dead or inanimate, is fair game as the object to be guessed, such as a fictional hero, a city in South America, or a current political figure. To be fair, there should be a reasonable chance that the game player will know about the object once it is identified.

The purpose is for the game player to deduce the answer using no more than 20 yes/no questions. Aficionados of the game become quite adept at asking questions that rapidly bracket in the object and

Exhibit 2.1

The Laboratory Arrangement for the Stooge Study

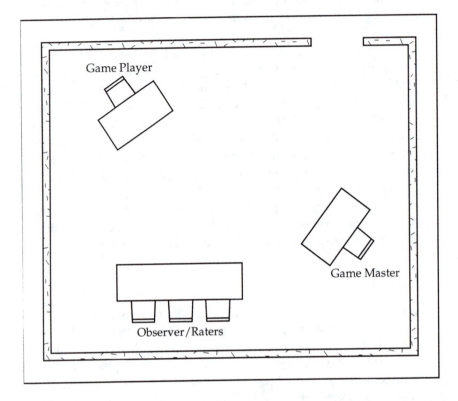

also at recognizing poor questioning strategy in the play of others. For example, a first question might be "Is it animal?" Either a *yes* or a *no* answer helps limit the field. To ask right off "Is it Elvis?" would likely just waste a question. If the "animal" question was answered *yes*, then the next question might be "Is it human?" Again, if *yes*, one could go on with "Currently living?" and so forth. To those not familiar with the game, it may seem impossible to bracket anything with just 20 questions, but in fact answers often are deduced with fewer than 20 well-chosen inquiries.

The subject who was seated in the lone chair was the first game player and then exchanged positions with one of the observer/raters. This rotation continued until all four had played the game. As each question was asked by the player, the others were instructed to rate that question on a scale of *very good* to *very poor* using a standard form provided by the game master. Questions could not be asked faster than one every 15 seconds so as to standardize pace and allow the observer/raters to keep up. The game master asked for each new question as it was due, and the game player had 5 seconds in which to ask it or forfeit that question.

The three observer/raters were not to talk to each other during the session. Therefore, during this part of the experiment, there was no social interaction among the subjects. They simply rotated through who was the game player, playing one game each, trying to guess the new object the game master had in mind. When they were observer/raters, they quietly observed and individually evaluated the questions being asked by whoever was the game player at that time. There was no group process as such during the game playing, only sets of three people watching and evaluating a fourth person. After all four had finished, they sat around and discussed game strategy for 10 minutes. Then each filled out a 12-item form rating each of the other three subjects and finally ranked the four players (including himself or herself) on who had contributed the best ideas to the discussion and who he or she liked best. These latter data provided supplementary evidence of the validity of the experiment.

Standardization of the situation was achieved in several ways. First, the game master used the same four objects to be guessed in each lab session. In fact, the game master role was entirely scripted: the same welcoming procedure, the same explanation of game rules, the same demeanor in responding to questions, and so forth. Second, and most important, the stooge role was also entirely scripted. For these data, the same male stooge was used in all sessions. He always seated himself in the center chair of the long table at the beginning so that he was between two naive subjects. Thus he was always third to play the game. He was always given the same topic to deduce and was trained to use the same set of 16 questions, word for word, every time; he always got the right answer on the 16th question. Consequently, the objective content of his performance was as nearly identical from one lab session to another as was humanly possible.

Sixteen sessions were run, involving 48 students from the same very large, undergraduate group behavior course. The stooge was taking that course also. Four treatments were employed, representing two variations in how neatly the stooge was dressed (neat vs. sloppy) and two variations in apparent confidence of the stooge while asking questions (confident vs. hesitant). In the confident role, the stooge gave the impression he was following an explicit strategy, had a good idea of what the object to be guessed was, and pretty much expected the game master's responses to the questions he asked. In the hesitant role, he appeared to be making vague guesses and to be somewhat baffled by the game master's responses. Remember, however, that identical questions were used by the stooge in all sessions. Subjects were randomly assigned to treatment so as to minimize the likelihood of any pretreatment differences among the groups.

All told, then, the experiment controlled the objective content of the stooge's behavior, the behavior of the game master, the setting, and the nonsocial character of the relationship between the naive subjects. Further, repetitions of each of the four variations were as nearly identical as possible, and differences among the variations were as great as possible. The intent, after all, was to remove or keep constant all factors that might impinge on the ratings given the stooge's questions except for the explicit manipulations of confidence and appearance. After each session, students were asked not to discuss the experiment with their classmates until all sessions had been run. Informal checks indicated that the request had been honored, and each batch of naive subjects apparently entered the experiment with no idea of what was to take place. Assuming that all of these procedures had their desired effect, there still remains the question of whether the particular sample of students who were naive subjects was in any way representative of students in general, young adults in general, or even people in general.

Results

With four sessions per treatment, there were 12 naive subject ratings of the stooge's questions for each treatment. Although the rating scale showed only 5 values (−2 for *very poor* to +2 for *very good*), subjects could place a check anywhere along the scale line, and fractional scores were assigned accordingly. This procedure provided essentially continuous measurement. Each subject's ratings for the 16 questions were averaged to provide one overall subject rating of the stooge in that treatment. Thus there was one overall rating from each of the 12 naive subjects in each treatment; these 48 overall ratings are the basic data of the experiment.

Exhibit 2.2

Basic Results of the Stooge Experiments

Treatment	Mean Rating
Confident-Sloppy	0.43
Confident-Neat	0.39
Hesitant-Neat	−0.05
Hesitant-Sloppy	−0.34

The simplest approach to answering the question of whether the treatments had different effects on stooge rating is to average the 12 overall subject ratings for each treatment and then compare those averages across the treatments. The resulting mean ratings for the four treatments are shown in Exhibit 2.2. Did appearance and apparent confidence alter how others judged the presumably objective quality of the questions the stooge asked? The impression from Exhibit 2.2 is that variation in dress and confidence did affect ratings of the stooge's questions. The total range of the rating scale was 4 points (−2 to +2), and so a difference between the mean of the "confident-sloppy" role (.43) and the mean of the "hesitant-sloppy" role (−.34) is nearly one fifth of the total scale range.

How Do We Interpret the Results?

Before being concerned with statistical analysis of the results of an experiment, such as the numbers in Exhibit 2.2, we should consider carefully whether the experiment was designed in such a way that we can trust those results. As you know, there are several considerations in designing valid and informative experiments. Remember the three major criteria: manipulation, control, and random assignment. The question of manipulation concerns not only how the stimuli are altered from treatment to treatment but also whether that manipulation was successful. The question of control is how, and how successfully, selected factors were held constant or at least how their influence was minimized. The question of random assignment is simply whether pure chance is the basis for any given subject being assigned to a particular treatment.

Other questions need also be considered in evaluating an experiment such as how results are measured, whether experimental procedures introduce biases into the results, how the sample of subjects is drawn, and how big the sample is. These concerns can be grouped primarily into questions about the validity of the experiment and questions about our confidence in statistical interpretations of the results. You should think back over the material in Chapter 1 and the description of the experiment just provided to ask yourself whether you see any problems in the experimental design and to consider how you might have done it better. From the distance of years, it is apparent that some things could have been done differently, but the critique will be left up to you. The point of describing the stooge study in detail is to provide a continuing example for illustrating the variations of ANOVA to be presented in subsequent chapters.

The statistical questions to be addressed are (a) whether we should conclude that the treatment affected stooge ratings and (b) how confident we can be in our conclusion. To discuss such matters involves both terminology and logic that you no doubt have learned previously. Because such knowledge has a sneaky way of evaporating when not in use, it will help to review some basic principles of statistical inference before turning to the principles of analyzing experimental results.

Problems of Statistical Inference

The main statistical question for the stooge experiment is "Are the differences in Exhibit 2.2 large enough that we can feel justified in stating that the 'irrelevant' aspects of stooge behavior were relevant after all?" This is not as simple a question as it appears at first. One possible interpretation would be that the different treatment means were unique to the particular subjects we studied and have little to do with how anyone else would behave. The question comes down to whether the responses from these particular students represent how any larger population of people would respond in the same situation. Obviously, this problem has to do with sampling. Actually, there are two problems. The first is whether we have sampled properly from the population about which we want to theorize. This is both a theoretical and a methodological problem. The second is to what extent we might by chance select a sample that misrepresents the "truth" about that population.

About Samples and Populations

Let's be clear about the terms *sample* and *population*. A population consists of all possible cases of a particular kind such as all students, all task-oriented small groups, all cities with more than 100,000 inhabitants in the United States, or all international corporations. We might not even know how many cases there are "out there," but we have conceptualized the population and wish to describe it, understand it, and maybe even be able to control certain aspects of it. It is important to realize that a population is an abstraction meant to stand for an entire set of empirical realities of a given kind that we assume is out there. If we could measure all cases in whatever population about which we wish to theorize, then life would be much simpler, but that is almost invariably impossible.

A sample is a particular set of cases. We know they are there because we observe them, measure them, or otherwise obtain data about them. If we have selected a sample properly, then we can expect that, at least on the average, the cases will represent reasonably well the total population from which they come. But any particular sample might in fact misrepresent the population for various reasons. Let's distinguish two types of representativeness: *conceptual* and *statistical*. Conceptually, a sample represents a population if the cases drawn into the sample can potentially be any of the types of cases found in the population. Selecting only Protestants would not be conceptually representative of those who are religious; selecting only students would not be conceptually representative of all people.

Returning to the stooge experiment, if we had run all possible people as experimental subjects, then we could simply look at the data and state with complete assurance that there are real differences in mean response to the four combinations of confidence and appearance. But what does "all possible people" mean? All students in that class? All students anywhere? Everyone currently alive? Obviously, there is no way we could study everyone in such large populations. For almost all social research, we need to study a sample of cases and hope that our results can be generalized to the population we have in mind.

Immediately it becomes necessary to specify what population we want to discuss. If our hypothesis is assumed to apply to all humans, then we would need to have sampled all types of people: races, nationalities, ages, genders, perhaps even historical eras. Of course, that is not possible. We could never finish just this one simple project. Instead, we took a sample of students and hoped that the sample would represent the population to which we want our hypothesis to apply.

Now, we used only students in a particular class from a particular university during a particular year. Is this sample conceptually representative of people in general? Can we assume that the full range of people will respond as those students did? Much theory about human behavior has in fact relied on studies of university students only. Sometimes it seems reasonable to generalize beyond the student populations sampled, but other times that seems very inappropriate. For example, students seldom are representative of overall political attitudes in any country at any time, but they may be quite broadly representative in terms of, say, the principles of operant psychology.

We might have temporarily resolved this problem at the outset by stating that a *boundary condition* of the hypothesis is that it applies only to undergraduate students. Boundary conditions are limitations placed on the assumed applicability of a hypothesis or theory. For example, much theory about small-group decision making explicitly applies only to what are called task-oriented groups. The advantage of specifying such a boundary condition is that our problem of representativeness would be reduced to whether the students we selected represented undergraduate students in general. That might be a reasonable assumption, although we do know that some characteristics of student populations vary regionally in the United States and certainly internationally. Fortunately, we often can check such an assumption by obtaining a variety of data from our subjects that can be compared against what is known about students more widely.

The disadvantage of stating such a narrow boundary condition would be that we would be developing a theory of undergraduate students, not of people in general. On the other hand, if we wish to hypothesize about people in general, then we would have to hold these particular results as very tentative until we did similar experiments with other types of subjects. The point is that our data are from a unique set of people: one particular sample. Drawing conclusions from those data depends on how well the sample conceptually represents the population: the total set of cases to which our hypothesis or theory should apply.

Even if the sample contains all the types of cases about which we wish to theorize, there still is the possibility that the sample does not represent that population *statistically*. Any particular sample is just one of the possible samples (i.e., the possible sets of cases) from the population. For example, if we took a sample of 5 students from a seminar in which 10 students were enrolled, we could get 252 different combinations of students, or 252 different samples. Obviously, if we take 1 sample, then we end up with only 1 of those possible samples. If we select cases into our sample randomly, then each 1 of those 252 possible samples would be equally likely. Suppose, for convenience, that we wanted to use the average height of the sample (our randomly selected 5 cases) to represent average height of the population (all 10 students). By pure chance, we could have gotten the 5 tallest people in the class, or the 5 shortest, or some other nonrepresentative set of 5 cases. How can we possibly conclude anything about the population if we could be so wrong?

Two Important Statistical Principles

Fortunately, there are some statistical principles that help us make conclusions. The important question is not whether a given sample *is* representative; we can never answer that question unless we know all about the population. If that were the case, then studying the sample would be a waste of time. The important question is what is the *chance* (or probability) that the sample provides misleading data? It is always possible to get a nonrepresentative sample using proper sampling methods, although there are detailed sampling procedures that minimize the chance of nonrepresentativeness. Regardless, if we use random sampling methods, then we can estimate the chance that our sample data are misleading. Consider the following two well-known principles.

> *The Law of Large Numbers* Informally stated, this "law" says that as the number of cases in a random sample increases, the probability that a sample mean will deviate from the population mean decreases.

The Law of Large Numbers is not just a conjecture; it can be proven mathematically and demonstrated beyond any question by computer simulation methods.

Exhibit 2.3

Sampling Distributions for Samples of Size 2 From a Population With Values 1, 2, 3, 4, and 5

Individual Sample	Mean	Probabilities
1,1	1.0	.04
1,2 2,1	1.5	.08
1,3 2,2 3,1	2.0	.12
1,4 2,3 3,2 4,1	2.5	.16
1,5 2,4 3,3 4,2 5,1	3.0	.20
2,5 3,4 4,3 5,2	3.5	.16
3,5 4,4 5,3	4.0	.12
4,5 5,4	4.5	.08
5,5	5.0	.04

Remember that any statistic, like the sample mean, has a *sampling distribution*. The sampling distribution for a sample mean refers to the set of possible values the sample mean can have and the chance of getting each of those values in the sample that we select. An extreme sample mean (way off from the true population mean) will have little chance of occurring randomly. A sample mean close to the true population mean will have quite a large chance of occurring randomly. The Law of Large Numbers, then, assures us that as sample size increases, the extent to which the sample mean will vary around the true population mean decreases. That is equivalent to stating that the *variance* of the sampling distribution decreases as sample size increases. For a small sample, the set of possible sample means can vary widely around the true population mean, μ. For a very large sample, the set of possible sample means will be clustered increasingly tightly around the true population mean, μ. The bigger the sample, the less chance we have of getting a seriously misleading result due solely to random sampling.

Exhibit 2.3 shows the sampling distribution for a very simple sampling problem. Suppose the population consists of only five cases and that those cases have values on some variable, Y; for convenience, the values of Y are 1, 2, 3, 4, and 5 for the five cases, respectively. What is the sampling distribution of the mean of samples of size 2? If we allow the same case to be drawn twice in a given sample (what is called *replacement sampling*), and if we keep track of the order in which cases are drawn into the sample, then there are

Exhibit 2.4

Sampling Distribution for Samples of Size 3 From a Population With Values 1, 2, 3, 4, and 5

Mean	Probability
1.00	.008
1.33	.024
1.67	.048
2.00	.080
2.33	.120
2.67	.144
3.00	.152
3.33	.144
3.67	.120
4.00	.080
4.33	.048
4.67	.024
5.00	.008

25 different samples we can get. Each of them will have exactly the same probability of being drawn if cases are drawn randomly: $\frac{1}{25}$ or .04. Some of them have the same mean, however, and so they are grouped together in Exhibit 2.3.

The sum of the probabilities in Exhibit 2.3 equals 1.0, which means that all possible results are accounted for. With the values of 1, 2, 3, 4, and 5 in the population, it is easy to see that the population mean, μ, equals 3.0. Now note that the samples with means close to μ occur more frequently than do those with more extreme values. Next, look at Exhibit 2.4, which is the sampling distribution for samples of size 3 (i.e., for $n = 3$) from the same population of five cases. Because there now are 125 possible samples (assuming replacement sampling and keeping track of order of selection), the individual samples are not listed but the probabilities accurately represent what those 125 possible samples would show.

Check two things about Exhibit 2.4 versus Exhibit 2.3. First, the samples are clustered a little more tightly around the true population mean. For $n = 2$ (Exhibit 2.3), 76% of the samples have means between 2.0 and 4.0 inclusive, or within 1 unit of the true mean. For $n = 3$ (Exhibit 2.4), 84% of the samples have means between 2.0 and 4.0. This is not a huge change, but it does illustrate the Law of Large

Numbers: As sample size increases, a larger proportion of the samples has means close to the population mean.

The second fact to note in comparing the two sampling distributions is that if you draw a graph of each, the shapes will be somewhat different. For Exhibit 2.3, you will get a perfect triangle with its peak at the population mean of 3.00. For Exhibit 2.4, the graph will first accelerate and then taper off across values close to the population mean of 3.00; it will repeat that process in reverse as you go to means beyond 3.00. In fact, the curve begins to look something like a normal curve.

Increasing sample size to $n = 4$ (again with replacement and distinguishing possible orders of selection) means that we now can get 625 different samples. That is too many to show in an exhibit. However, calculating exact probabilities of each possible sample mean shows that now there will be 88.8% of the samples having means between 2.0 and 4.0. Again, as the sample size increases, the chance of getting a particularly misleading sample decreases. If fact, for $n = 4$, there is less than half the chance of getting a sample mean more than 1 unit away from μ (a probability of .112) than there is for $n = 2$ (a probability of .24). Exhibit 2.5 shows graphs of the three different curves. The line for $n = 2$ may look higher at the mean, but the curve is much broader than it is for $n = 3$ or $n = 4$. As n increases, the curve clusters more tightly around μ.

The second point noted in comparing the $n = 2$ distribution to the $n = 3$ distribution is that a graph of the probabilities of each possible sample mean shows a more normal-looking curve for the larger sample. Graphing all three sampling distributions, as is shown in Exhibit 2.5, illustrates that fact more clearly. That brings us to the second important principle: the Central Limit Theorem.

Remember that a sample mean is simply a sum of values divided by the number of cases in the sample. When a sample is randomly selected, the sum of values for the variable being measured *is* the sum of a set of random values from the population. If the distribution of the sum of values in the sample becomes increasingly normal, then the distribution of the sample mean necessarily also becomes increasingly normal. Therefore, the Central Limit Theorem tells us that as sample size increases, the sampling distribution of the sample mean (i.e., the distribution of possible sample means and the chance of getting each of those values) becomes increasingly normal.

Exhibit 2.5

Graphs of Sampling Distributions for *n* = 2, 3, and 4

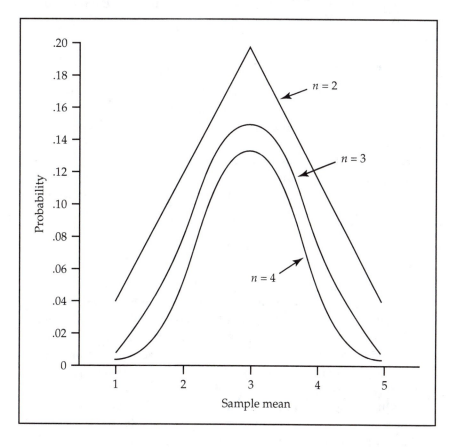

> ***The Central Limit Theorem*** Informally stated, this theorem
> says that the distribution of the sum of a set of random val-
> ues of a variable increasingly approaches a normal distribu-
> tion as the number of values in the sum increases.

We can use statistical tables or programs to find out exactly the
chance of getting any particular value from a normal distribution.
If our sample is large enough to warrant the assumption of normality, then we can estimate the chance of getting any particular range
of sample means. Taken together, the Law of Large Numbers and

the Central Limit Theorem assure us that, for large enough samples, we can make a fairly accurate estimate of the chance that our random sample is misleading by any given amount. That forms the basis for the logic of statistical inference.

On the Concept of Variance

Variance is a central concept for the logic underlying the kinds of statistical tests we will examine. Informally, that just sounds like how much some observations vary among themselves. Formally, as you undoubtedly recall from introductory statistics, the concept is the average squared deviation of a set of values from the mean. Sometimes the term *mean squared deviation* is used as synonymous with variance. If Y is the variable and μ is the population mean, then the variance is

$$\sigma_y^2 = \frac{1}{N} \sum_i (Y_i - \mu)^2. \qquad (2.1)$$

The subscript, i, simply indicates which case is being considered. For a population with N cases in it, we would take in turn the value of Y for each case, Y_i, subtract the population mean, $(Y_i - \mu)$, square that difference, $(Y_i - \mu)^2$, add up those squared differences over all cases, and divide by the number of cases. There is a more convenient computational form of the equation for variance, but for now the definitional form will suffice.

Although the informal statement of the Law of Large Numbers that was provided previously says nothing about variance as such, there is a very precise relationship between the population variance and the variance of the sampling distribution of the sample mean. That relationship is

$$\sigma_{\bar{Y}}^2 = \frac{\sigma_y^2}{n}. \qquad (2.2)$$

As the sample size increases, the variance of the sampling distribution of the sample mean decreases proportionately. The importance of this convenient fact for present purposes is that if we know the variance of the sampling distribution of sample means, then we can calculate the variance of the population.

In practice, we cannot expect to know either the population or the sampling distribution variance. If we did, we would not need to study a sample. However, we can estimate the population variance based on sample data. We can also estimate the population variance by looking at the variance of sample means and using that as an estimate of the variance of the sampling distribution of means under the assumption that the samples all came from populations with the same mean. That assumption amounts to saying that the experimental manipulation had no effect: that stooge appearance and performance did not affect evaluations of the stooge's questions.

The crux of the logic of ANOVA is to estimate the population variance by these two independent methods, one of which is based on the hypothesis under analysis and the other of which is independent of that hypothesis, and compare those estimates to see whether they agree. Do not be disconcerted if that does not seem crystal clear at the moment. The logic will be developed in detail as we proceed. The important point for now is that variance is *the* central concept throughout this book. We will simply look at various ways in which to estimate variance, and those estimates involve different hypotheses that try to account for observed variation in the data. The comparison of different estimates of variance constitutes the basis for a statistical test known as an *F* test. It will be useful at this point to review the logic of statistical tests.

Conducting Formal Tests

For the stooge data, we had four treatments with a sample of 12 observations for each treatment. If, for samples of this size, we could expect the sample means to vary widely (i.e., the sampling distribution to have a large variance), then maybe any observed differences among the means are just due to random sampling fluctuation. On the other hand, if the variance of the sampling distribution of sample means is small, then we might conclude that it is very unlikely that the observed differences among treatment means arose simply through random sampling fluctuation.

To test the hypothesis that behavior and appearance can influence evaluations requires first stating that hypothesis carefully so that we know just what we are testing. The hypothesis has both a substantive and a statistical form, and typically it is stated in null, or "no difference," form. That is not always the optimal approach, but it is the best way in which to introduce the subject of statistical testing. Substantively, the null hypothesis would be that the four treatments make absolutely no difference in how people evaluate the questions asked by the stooge. Statistically, that amounts to the hypothesis that the means of the populations of people experiencing the different treatments all will be equal. In formal equation form, the statistical hypothesis is expressed as

$$\text{Hypothesis:} \quad \mu_{cs} = \mu_{cn} = \mu_{hs} = \mu_{hn},$$

where the subscripts represent the four different treatments (confident-sloppy [cs], confident-neat [cn], etc.). Note that this hypothesis pertains to the populations, that is, to the conceptual sets of all people faced with a given behavior-appearance combination.

Assume that we can estimate the probability that observed differences would have occurred due to random sampling alone if the null hypothesis were true. Obviously, if the observed treatment means differ substantially, and if there is little chance that those observed differences are due simply to random sampling, then it is very unlikely that the populations really have the same mean. That is, the experimental evidence is unlikely under the null hypothesis, and so it is plausible to argue that the treatments really do evoke differential responses. You may have to think that over a bit, but the logic is sound.

A formal statistical decision process involves not only stating the hypothesis but also deciding what chance we will be willing to take of making an erroneous decision. Of course, virtually any set of results could happen even if the null hypothesis is true. It is just that more extreme results become very unlikely, especially with larger samples. The less likely our results under a specified hypothesis, the more we should doubt that hypothesis. Note, however, that if the null hypothesis were in fact true and we happened by chance to get very unlikely results, then we would end up rejecting a true hypothesis. That would be erroneous; such an error has been called a Type I error.

Type I error is rejecting a true hypothesis.

We cannot know whether we are right or not, but we can decide what chance we will take of making a Type I error. When we establish the chance we are willing to take, we set α (Greek alpha, the standard symbol for the probability of Type I error) accordingly. Common values of α are .05 and .01, although the actual values chosen may depend on considerations such as the desirability of following up on promising leads (somewhat larger α values) versus the importance of rejecting well-established hypotheses only if evidence is overwhelming (small α values).

Having established what chance we will take of making a Type I error, we look at the actual data and calculate the probability that we would have gotten those results if the null hypothesis were true. When our calculations say the results are less likely than α, we formally reject the hypothesis. For the stooge data, suppose that we adopted the conventional 5% chance of incorrectly rejecting the null hypothesis, that is, α = .05. We then calculate the chance of finding treatment means that differ as much as those shown in Exhibit 2.2 if the null hypothesis were really true—if the populations really did not differ. How we do the calculations for various types of research design constitutes the major part of this book.

Whenever our calculations lead us to formally reject the null hypothesis, we conclude that the alternate hypothesis must be true. The population means really do differ; the treatments do have differential effects. If the results are more likely than α under the null hypothesis, then we do not reject the null hypothesis.

Not rejecting the hypothesis brings up the possibility of committing a Type II error. If the experimental manipulations actually are effective in the general population, but by chance we got an odd sample that did not respond typically, then the differences between the treatment means could be too small to reject the hypothesis even though it was true for the population.

Type II error is accepting a false hypothesis.

Many researchers do not formally reject or accept hypotheses; they simply report the probability of the results under the null hypothesis and allow readers to reach their own conclusions. For much general research, that makes good sense because one study alone is not an adequate basis for keeping or throwing out ideas. In applied research, however, it sometimes is necessary to make formal decisions. Does a corporation adopt a new technology or stick with the old? At some point, the decision makers have to decide whether evidence (usually experimental) warrants the change or not.

We will adopt the formal decision-making approach in this text. The steps are as follows:

1. State a testable statistical hypothesis.
2. Establish α.
3. Conduct an appropriate experiment (or other research project) to gather evidence.
4. Determine the likelihood of getting the observed results if the hypothesis were true.
5. If the likelihood is less than or equal to α, then reject the hypothesis. If the likelihood is greater than α, then accept it.

Keep in mind that others studying the same problem and even using the same procedures may not reach the same conclusions. Science is a cumulative process, one of sorting out the ideas that consistently gain empirical support from those that do not seem consistently compatible with observations. In any event, it is necessary to work out methods for two crucial steps in the overall research process once a hypothesis or set of hypotheses has been established.

The first step, assuming that we intend to do experiments, is to design them so that they will provide data relevant to our hypothesis. The second step is to estimate the probability that observed results would have occurred by chance if the null hypothesis is true. The first step was the subject of Chapter 1, but the particular form of experiment will vary depending on the hypotheses to be tested. For the second step, we will need to develop variations on the logic of the ANOVA and the use of an F test, which in turn will depend on the chosen experimental design.

About the F Test

The F test will be used throughout the variations of ANOVA that we will develop. You may have encountered the F distribution before but probably have not had any reason to connect it to other probability distributions you have used, in particular the normal, chi-square, and t distributions. This final short section of Chapter 2 sketches how those distributions are related so that you can connect the F test to other tests already familiar to you.

You no doubt already know what the normal distribution is like. It has that nice symmetrical shape that looks like a mountain in the distance or perhaps a mound of ice cream that went soft. Assume that you have some continuous variable, Y. If Y is normally distributed, then the chance of finding any particular value or range of values of Y depends on the specific normal distribution from which Y comes. Actually, there is an infinite number of possible normal distributions, but they all share the same formula. It depends entirely on just two parameters, or constants. Those parameters represent the two most important facts about any statistical population: its mean, μ, and its standard deviation, σ.

You can standardize a normal distribution by subtracting the mean from each value of Y and dividing that difference by the standard deviation. When Y is so standardized, it is called a *standard normal deviate*, usually represented by the letter z. There is only one standard normal distribution.

$$z = \frac{(Y - \mu)}{\sigma}. \tag{2.3}$$

Theoretically, you cannot determine the probability of randomly finding any single value of Y because, with continuous variables, there are only infinitesimal changes in Y across its entire range. However, you can determine the probability of randomly selecting a case with a value of Y between any two bounds, such as "What is the chance of randomly drawing a case with a value of Y between 10 and 15?" If we knew that Y was normally distributed in the population, with mean $\mu = 10$ and standard deviation $\sigma = 2.5$, then it would be easy to see that the associated z scores will be 0 and 2: $(10 - 10)/2.5 = 0$ and $(15 - 10)/2.5 = 2$. Then we could check the normal table for the chance of finding a standardized value between 0 and 2. That probability happens to be .4772, but we will not need the normal curve for ANOVA.

Whereas the normal distribution concerns only a single event (the chance of getting Y between 10 and 15), the chi-square distribution concerns a set of independent events. Suppose we select a sample of 25 cases from a population in which some property, Y, is normally distributed. If we know μ and σ, then we could convert all of the Y values to z scores, square them, and add them up. The sum of such a set of squared, standard, normal deviate scores will have a probability distribution described by the theoretical chi-square distribution.

So who cares? Why would we want to go through those steps? In fact, when a variance is calculated, we do all of that except dividing by σ. Remember that a variance formula is

$$\sigma_y^2 = \frac{\sum (Y - \mu)^2}{N}. \tag{2.4}$$

Let's concentrate on the numerator of the formula for variance. That is called a *sum of squares*, short for *sum of squared deviations about the mean*. Now, by taking each Y, subtracting μ, squaring the difference, and adding up over cases, we have almost created a sum of squared z scores. If a sample of n cases was randomly selected from the population and we calculated the sum of squares for the sample of Y values, then that sum will have a sampling distribution. That is, if you consider all possible samples of size n, the sum of squares will vary randomly from one possible sample to another. Each possible sum has a unique probability, and that probability can be determined by using the chi-square distribution. Dividing the sum of squares by a constant will not change the shape of its probability distribution. Therefore, sample estimates of the population variance will have sampling distributions that are described by the chi-square distribution.

It is not necessary to understand the mathematics of these formal distributions to get the point that variances involve calculating a sum of squares, and sums of squares have chi-square probability distributions, and so variances have chi-square distributions. However, as noted previously, the normal distribution concerns only one case. With variance and the chi-square distribution, however, we have a sample of n cases.

Now comes an important concept: *degrees of freedom*, or *df* for short. We will need to understand degrees of freedom when using ANOVA. Typically, we do not know the values of the population parameters such as μ. However, we can substitute the sample mean as an estimate of μ. Any time we estimate a parameter, such as using the sample mean in place of the population mean, we make redundant some of the information contained in the n separate cases drawn into the sample. Therefore, the number of cases with "free" information, or the degrees of freedom, is reduced by 1.

If someone had selected a sample of five values of Y, calculated the mean of those values, and told you the mean and the first four values, then you could figure out what the fifth value had to be. Suppose the first four values were 1, 4, 6, and 9, with a mean for all

5 values equal to 7. Then the fifth value would have to equal 15 so that the sum would be 35, giving a mean of 7. That last value becomes redundant once you know the first $n - 1$ values and the mean. This is the sense in which degrees of freedom refers to the number of cases in the sample that provide nonredundant information. If we used redundant information from a sample in estimating a population parameter, then we would get a biased estimate.

As an unbiased estimator of the population variance, a sample variance takes the form

$$s_y^2 = \frac{\sum (Y - \bar{Y})^2}{n - 1}. \tag{2.5}$$

Note that the denominator is $n - 1$, the *df*. The chi-square distribution depends on *df*, but remember that it pertains only to the sum of squares. A simple variation is called the *chi-square over df* distribution, which is appropriate for the sampling distribution of an estimate of variance, s^2.

For ANOVA, we will have to compare two independent estimates of the same variance. If they agree, then we will have confidence in our null hypothesis; if not, then we may choose to discard that hypothesis. We know that the sampling distribution for each estimate will be a chi-square distribution. How do we compare two such estimates? First, let's look at a messy equation showing a ratio of two estimates: s_1^2, *based on df_1 degrees of freedom, and s_2^2, based on df_2 degrees of freedom*. Do not be disconcerted by the double subscript on the Y terms. As before, i indicates which case. The number 1 or 2, throughout the equation, indicates sample 1 versus sample 2.

$$\frac{s_1^2}{s_2^2} = \frac{\dfrac{\sum (Y_{i1} - \bar{Y}_1)^2}{n_1 - 1}}{\dfrac{\sum (Y_{i2} - \bar{Y}_2)^2}{n_2 - 1}}. \tag{2.6}$$

The numerator of the right side of this terrible-looking expression is a sample estimate of variance based on n_1 cases. It would have a chi-square over *df* sampling distribution with $n_1 - 1$ *df*. Similarly, the denominator would have a chi-square over *df* sampling distribution with $n_2 - 1$ *df*. Because each of these terms has a sampling distribution, the terms' ratio also has a sampling distribution. It is more complicated because it depends on two different degrees of freedom. Fortunately, the F distribution is exactly what we need. It is the sampling distribution for the ratio of two chi-square over df distributions. Consequently, it is also the sampling distribution for the ratio of two independent estimates of the same population variance.

The essence of ANOVA is to make two different estimates of the population variance. One estimate will be dependent on the hypothesis under consideration, and the other will be independent of that hypothesis. By making a ratio of those two estimates, we will get a statistic that has an F distribution. There are two further points worth noting. Because F is a ratio of two independent chi-square over df distributions, and because chi-square is a distribution of the sum of independent, squared normal deviates, it follows that F depends on the dependent variable in question being normally distributed. (Actually, the deviations of individual values of Y around appropriate population means must satisfy normality.) It also follows that random sampling of independently selected cases underlies the applicability of the F distribution.

Summary

This chapter began with a description of the stooge experiment, a relatively simple example that will provide the basis for developing the logic of ANOVA. Before proceeding with that logic, however, it was necessary to review a number of statistical concepts. Populations are entire sets of cases "out there" that we wish our theory to address. Because we typically cannot study entire populations, we select samples that we hope represent those populations. We cannot guarantee that a sample will be representative, but two statistical principles form the basis for being able to estimate the likelihood that our sample will mislead us. Those principles are the Law of Large Numbers and the Central Limit Theorem.

The concept of a sampling distribution, which is essential to the logic of statistical testing, was then discussed. Some researchers use formal tests that result in explicit acceptance or rejection of a hypothesis, whereas others simply estimate and report the probability that observed data would be found if a hypothesis were true. In either case, sampling distributions and variances are crucial parts of the statistical logic. A brief excursion traced the idea of a normal distribution to a chi-square distribution appropriate as the sampling distribution for a single estimate of a population variance, to an F distribution as the sampling distribution for the ratio of two independent estimates of the same population variance. ANOVA involves making one estimate of variance based on the hypothesis being tested and an independent estimate not based on that hypothesis. Determining whether those estimates agree is the crux of ANOVA. Therefore, the F distribution is central to the ANOVA.

There are many useful texts that discuss many of the ideas presented in this chapter. You might want to consult Arney (1990), Estes (1991), Jaccard and Becker (1990), and Loether and McTavish (1993).

Notes

1. The stooge who contributed so much to our earlier investigations was Sheila A. Selfors. For the past 27 years, she has been Sheila Leik.
2. A full description of procedures and results appears in Leik (1965a).

3 One-Way Analysis of Variance

The basic question in ANOVA is whether, on the average, two or more populations are different on some dependent variable. That question is answered by appropriate calculations using sample data. This chapter is intended to help you understand (a) how the calculations for the simplest version of ANOVA are done and interpreted, (b) whether you can reach a conclusion that the populations are or are not significantly different, and (c) how confident you can be that such a conclusion is valid. It is, of course, possible to conduct ANOVA without knowing why the various numbers involved are calculated or what justifies the conclusion about group differences. There are several problems with not understanding what is behind the calculations. The two most critical ones are as follows:

1. There are many variations of ANOVA, each suited to a particular set of research operations. You need to understand the different models on which those variations are based and what assumptions they make to tailor ANOVA to your research needs.

2. If your research situation does not match exactly the assumptions of one of the standard ANOVA variations, then you need to know how to decide whether or not to trust the results.

In a nutshell, if you do not understand why a statistical procedure works (and when it does not work), then you might reach totally inappropriate research conclusions without knowing it. Not only would that be a waste of your time, but it could get pretty embarrassing when someone else discovers your goof.

Some Fundamental Formalities

Before getting tangled in equations, let's review the terminology and notation needed for ANOVA. This can be prosaic, but it is the only way in which you are able to work back and forth between the substantive theory you want to test and the data you get from your research.

Terminology and Notation

It is assumed that there is one interval-level *dependent* variable on which a set of groups is being compared and at least one nominal-level *independent* variable (usually called a *factor*) on which the groups are based. Remember that *nominal* measurement means simply an unordered set of categories or classes. You cannot add or subtract nominal variables; just use them to sort cases. *Interval* (short for *equal interval*) variables use standardized units of measurement that do allow for addition and subtraction. The stooge experiment described in chapter 2 had a dependent variable measured by having subjects place a check mark on a continuous line with clearly marked equal intervals. It generally is agreed that such a procedure produces data satisfying the equal interval criterion. The independent variable was treatment: one of four distinct, unordered categories of experience in the lab.

An experiment is designed to enable manipulation of the factor (or factors) that constitutes the independent variable(s), and it produces information about the interval-level dependent variable(s) for a sample of cases studied. Initially, we will discuss experiments with just one factor (e.g., one set of distinct unordered types of treatment) and just one dependent variable (e.g., stooge rating). We can consider adding more factors later. We will also assume that the dependent variable will be measured only once, after the experimental treatment. Given our simple one-factor problem, then, each case in the sample will have one group or factor value (which experimental treatment group that case was in) and one value of the dependent variable. The entire data set for this simplest design will consist of a case number, a group or treatment number, X, and a value of the dependent variable, Y, for each of the n cases in the sample.

To keep track of which case is being referred to in the equations that follow, Y needs the case number as a subscript. That is, Y_1 will refer to the value of Y for case 1. However, we often want to refer to a general case rather than to a specific one when we are working out the equations for ANOVA, and so the letter i will be used as a general subscript. It is usual to define Y and its subscripts formally as

$$Y_i; i = 1 .. n,$$

which means that Y_i refers to the value of Y for any general case, i, and i can take on any value from 1 to n. Assuming that there are n cases in our sample, we have a general way of referring to any or all of those cases.

It will also be necessary to keep track of which treatment a case has experienced, that is, which value of the factor applies to that case. A second subscript will do that job. (Do not panic; that is almost as complicated as it gets in this book.) If there were three experimental treatments, for example, then the second subscript would take on a value of 1, 2, or 3. As with denoting cases, we often want a general subscript for groups and will use the letter j for that purpose.

Now comes a sometimes confusing but very convenient convention. It should be obvious that all the cases with the same value on the factor belong to the same group. Everyone who experienced treatment 1 would be in group 1, everyone having treatment 2 would be in group 2, and so on. Because the second subscript identifies which group the case is in, the first subscript can now refer specifically to cases only in that group. For example, $Y_{5,2}$ means the value of the dependent variable for the fifth case in group 2.

Again formally, the double subscripting would be stated as

$$Y_{i,j}; i = 1 .. n_j, j = 1 .. J,$$

where n_j is the number of cases in group j and J is the number of groups. It follows that there will be a case 1 for each group, indicating the first case in that group. The highest value that the subscript i can take on will be the size of the group to which that case belongs, or n_j.

It may help to use this notation with some specific data, and so we will look at the actual data from the stooge study. They are shown in Exhibit 3.1. Recall that the dependent variable, Y, is each naive subject's postdiscussion rating of the value of the stooge's contributions. To make it easier to get a sense of the data, the case numbers have been rearranged so that entries in Exhibit 3.1 go from highest to lowest. Of course, the actual values did not show such a convenient ordering.

The entries under the case number column tell us which cases we are looking at. For each group, there are 12 cases. Remember, this does not mean that there were 12 people in a single lab session; rather, it tells us that for any given treatment, we ran 4 sessions with 3 naive subjects per session, giving 12 cases per treatment group.

Exhibit 3.1

Stooge Ratings by Treatment

	Value of Y Ratings of Stooge's Contributions			
	Group 1	Group 2	Group 3	Group 4
Case Number	(neat-confident)	(neat-hesitant)	(sloppy-confident)	(sloppy-hesitant)
1	$Y_{1,1} = 1.50$	$Y_{1,2} = 1.00$	$Y_{1,3} = 1.50$	$Y_{1,4} = .50$
2	$Y_{2,1} = 1.25$	$Y_{2,2} = .50$	$Y_{2,3} = 1.25$	$Y_{2,4} = .27$
3	$Y_{3,1} = 1.00$	$Y_{3,2} = .50$	$Y_{3,3} = 1.00$	$Y_{3,4} = 0$
4	$Y_{4,1} = .75$	$Y_{4,2} = 0$	$Y_{4,3} = 1.00$	$Y_{4,4} = 0$
5	$Y_{5,1} = .39$	$Y_{5,2} = 0$	$Y_{5,3} = .50$	$Y_{5,4} = 0$
6	$Y_{6,1} = 0$	$Y_{6,2} = 0$	$Y_{6,3} = 0$	$Y_{6,4} = 0$
7	$Y_{7,1} = 0$	$Y_{7,2} = 0$	$Y_{7,3} = 0$	$Y_{7,4} = -.34$
8	$Y_{8,1} = 0$	$Y_{8,2} = 0$	$Y_{8,3} = 0$	$Y_{8,4} = -.40$
9	$Y_{9,1} = 0$	$Y_{9,2} = -.08$	$Y_{9,3} = 0$	$Y_{9,4} = -.89$
10	$Y_{10,1} = 0$	$Y_{10,2} = -.50$	$Y_{10,3} = 0$	$Y_{10,4} = -1.00$
11	$Y_{11,1} = 0$	$Y_{11,2} = -1.00$	$Y_{11,3} = 0$	$Y_{11,4} = -1.00$
12	$Y_{12,1} = -.25$	$Y_{12,2} = -1.00$	$Y_{12,3} = -.10$	$12,4 = -1.27$

Group number, or X, is shown at the top of each column: group 1, 2, 3, or 4. Because Y is our dependent variable, values of Y are the entries shown for each case in each of the group columns. This may seem like excessive attention to notation and interpretation of the table, but these seemingly little things often cause confusion at first. Sometime in the future when you set up your own data, you have to be absolutely sure what the entries are all about.

Formal notation is shown in the following for three entries in Exhibit 3.1. Be sure that you understand what the subscripts mean and why each of the values shown is correct, based on the table. Because the first subscript concerns which case in a group, it refers to which row of the table. The second subscript refers to which group, hence to which column of the table:

$Y_{1,1} = 1.50$ (first case in group 1, the neat-confident group)

$Y_{5,2} = 0$ (fifth case in group 2, the neat-hesitant group)

$Y_{9,4} = -.89$ (ninth case in group 4, the sloppy-hesitant group)

Once you understand the subscripts, it is easy to move to the general equations needed for ANOVA. First, some further notation will come in handy. Remember that data come from samples taken from the populations we wish to analyze. If we had data on the whole population, then we would not need statistical inference procedures like ANOVA (which would save a lot of students a lot of trouble).

To keep population and sample information separate, we need separate notation for each. In general, Greek letters are used for population facts (called parameters) and Roman letters for sample facts (called statistics). At the population level, the Greek letter μ (mu) represents the arithmetic mean. Therefore, at the population level,

μ denotes the overall population mean for variable Y and

μ_j denotes the population mean for group j on variable Y.

At the sample level,

$Y_{i,j}$ denotes the value of Y for the ith case in group j,

$\overline{Y}_{.j}$ denotes the mean of variable Y for group j, and

$\overline{Y}_{..}$ denotes the mean of Y for the total sample.

Note that when a group mean is indicated, the individual case subscript is irrelevant; all cases in the group are involved in a mean. Therefore, a dot is used in place of the case subscript for any group mean. Similarly, which group is irrelevant when the mean of the total sample is used; all cases and all groups are included in that mean. Therefore, a dot also appears in place of the group subscript for the grand mean.

There is one common exception to the Greek versus Roman letters. Throughout this book, n will refer to the number of cases in a sample and N to the number of cases in the corresponding population. Not all texts follow this distinction, but it helps when keeping track of sample size versus population size.

Modeling Effects in a One-Way ANOVA

Now that basic notation is established, let's create a formal model of how the stooge's role influenced the ratings others made of his or her performance. The basic question is why values of Y vary from case to case. Part of that variation might be purely random. Part of it might be systematic differences among the groups due to the experimental treatments actually having different effects. Our model will need to include systematic consequences of the experimental treatments plus randomness produced by, for example, sampling or measurement error. The statistical question that links the data to our theory concerns whether we can conclude that the treatment populations differ, on the average, based on variation among treatment group means from the sample data. If so, then the theory-based factor of *treatment* can be said to account for, or "explain," a portion of the overall variance of the dependent variable Y in the populations. The crucial idea is that we are trying to analyze variance at the *population* level.

Anything we cannot explain by treatment will, of course, remain unexplained because, with our very simple experimental design, treatment is the only way of explaining variance in the dependent variable. If systematic effects of other possible influences have been controlled by random assignment or boundary conditions, then all unexplained variance will be considered random "error." The term *error* in this usage explicitly means any deviation of an observed value of Y from what we would predict that value to be based on our theoretical model, and *random* means such deviation is assumed to be unrelated to anything else in the experiment.

If the experimental subjects are randomly assigned to treatment, then, *on the average*, the treatment groups ought to be alike before the experiment. From what we know about the sampling distribution of means, however, we can expect some random differences among group means even before the experiment begins. If the different experimental treatments do have different systematic effects, then, *on the average*, the treatment groups should differ after the experiment beyond any random variation in the means due to random assignment. That is, each specific treatment will have systematically added something to (or subtracted something from) each case's value of Y. Necessarily, then, the treatment effects will have increased the overall variance of Y.

Statistically, that means that after the experiment, each case value, $Y_{i,j}$, can be thought of as equal to the overall population mean, μ, plus that case's random (i.e., unexplained) deviation from the population mean, $e_{i,j}$, plus any systematic effect of treatment experienced by that case. It will not be necessary to include a group difference term from *before* the experiment if we are justified in assuming that, on the average, there were no such differences. Because treatments all are at the group level, we can denote treatment effects as group effects, β_j. Therefore,

$$Y_{i,j} = \mu + \beta_j + e_{i,j}. \tag{3.1}$$

Equation 3.1 can be read as follows. The value of Y for each case in each group in the population, $Y_{i,j}$, is a sum of three different effects: the overall mean of all cases in the total population, μ, a unique group effect for the particular group that case is in, β_j, and random variation due to chance or unknown influences on that particular case in that particular group, $e_{i,j}$.

Now consider the group-specific population mean for any group j prior to the effect of any experimental treatment. The β_j in Equation 3.1 will equal zero because there has been no treatment effect. Sum both sides of the equation over all cases in that group-specific population and divide by N_j, the number of cases. The left side of the equation will be the population mean, μ_j. The first part on the right side of the equation still will be μ. (Adding a constant N times and then dividing by N will equal that constant.) The second part of the right side will be the mean of the error terms.

If the sum of the $e_{i,j}$ is zero, then the group-specific population mean prior to experimental manipulations will equal the total population mean: $\mu_j = \mu$. Any other result would mean that the group differed from the total population for reasons having nothing to do with the experimental treatments. But our theoretical model assumes that the only reason for the groups to differ at the population level is the effects of our experimental manipulations: treatment effects. Without those systematic effects, the groups must have equal population means. Therefore, the individual random errors in the population average zero within any group.

At the group level, then, averaging over all cases in group j gives

$$\mu_j = \mu + \beta_j \tag{3.2}$$

because the errors average out to zero. Now suppose that the experimental treatments had no effect at all. Then $\beta_j = 0$ for all groups, and the group-specific population means all would be equal even after the experiment:

$$H_0: \mu_1 = \mu_2 = \mu_3 = \ldots = \mu_J = \mu. \tag{3.3}$$

Formally, this is the null hypothesis. It states in equation form that all the population means are the same; all are equal to the overall population mean. There are no group differences; hence the different treatments do not produce different results. The logical alternative to a null hypothesis is that at least some of the population means are different:

$$H_1: \mu_1 \neq \mu_2 \neq \mu_3. \tag{3.4}$$

Typically, it is assumed that either H_0 or H_1 is true because together they comprise all possibilities. If we conclude that one is false, then the other is true by implication. Actually, it would be possible for two of the means to be equal and the third to differ from both of them. Informally, you might interpret the two hypotheses as "On the average, the populations are the same" versus "No, they are not."

At the sample level, the *expected value* of the mean for group j, $\overline{Y}_{.j}$, is the population mean for that group, $\mu_{.j}$. The term *expected value*, as used here, refers to the mean of the sampling distribution. Any time a statistic is an *unbiased estimator* of a population parameter, the mean of its sampling distribution will equal that parameter. Because a sample mean is an unbiased estimator of the population mean, the expected value of each group sample mean will be the population mean for that group.

As we know, the *observed value* of any particular sample mean usually will differ from the population mean because of random sampling variation. For the data in Exhibit 3.1, the group means are +.39, −.05, +.43, and −.34. These are different, of course, but their differences might be due simply to random variation of the cases that make up the groups. The problem is how to decide whether the sample group means after the experiment differ enough to conclude that there are real effects of the treatments. If the means turn out to be identical (do not count on it; it never happens), then the conclusion that the treatment factor had no effect would seem obvious. However, as the concept of Type II error should tell you, even that conclusion could be wrong.

Exhibit 3.2 shows a graphic display of how the particular cases from Exhibit 3.1 are spread out. Each dot represents one case. The solid lines are drawn at the group means, and the dotted line represents the overall mean of all groups. Do you think that the groups look different enough to decide that the differences among their means are not just the result of random sampling fluctuation? At what point should we conclude that there must be nonzero β values because the observed group means differ too much to be attributable simply to fluctuation in the sampling distribution? Are .43 and −.34 far enough apart, given these small samples, to conclude that the groups were affected differently by the experimental treatments?

We need to compare variation *between* the groups to variation *within* the groups. If data vary a lot within the groups, then they vary a lot in the population. For relatively small samples, then, the sampling distribution of the means will be relatively large so that even large differences among group means could occur fairly often

Exhibit 3.2

Graphic Display of the Data From Exhibit 3.1

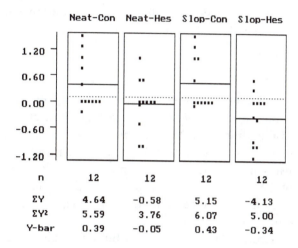

	Neat-Con	Neat-Hes	Slop-Con	Slop-Hes
n	12	12	12	12
ΣY	4.64	-0.58	5.15	-4.13
ΣY²	5.59	3.76	6.07	5.00
Y-bar	0.39	-0.05	0.43	-0.34

due purely to random sampling. On the other hand, if variation within the groups is quite small, then the sampling distribution of the sample means will be small and it will not take a lot of difference between observed sample means to convince us that systematic effects of the treatment are present.

It is important that you get a good intuitive sense of this comparison of variation among group means with variation within the groups. Keeping that idea in mind will make the more formal development of ANOVA much easier. Any observed differences among group means have to be judged in comparison with how much random error there is in the total population.

Sampling Distributions and Variance Estimates

The sampling distribution provides the basis for deciding how much each sample mean *might* be expected to vary around the overall mean *if* the null hypothesis that there are no group effects is true. Equation 2.2, from Chapter 2, expressed the relationship between the variance of a population and the variance of a sample mean for samples of size *n*:

$$\sigma_{\bar{Y}}^2 = \frac{\sigma_y^2}{n}.$$

Rearrange that expression by multiplying both sides by the sample size, n. It then says

$$n\,\sigma_{\bar{y}}^2 = n\,\frac{\sigma_y^2}{n},$$

or that the population variance is equal to the variance of the sampling distribution multiplied by sample size. If all of the sample means had the same sampling distribution, then things would be simple. We would need two steps. First, calculate the variance of the sample means around the overall mean of the sample data to get an estimate of the variance of the common sampling distribution. Second, multiply that variance estimate by sample size, n. The result would be a direct estimate of σ_y^2

Having a common sampling distribution would require three things. First, all of the sampling distributions of the sample means would have to have the same shape, or probability curve. As stated previously, if the samples are large enough or the populations themselves are normal, then all the sampling distributions will be normal, and this takes care of the shape criterion. For relatively small samples such as those in the stooge study, it will be necessary to assume population normality; each separate population must be normally distributed about its own mean. An equivalent statement is that the error terms, $e_{i,j}$, in Equation 3.1 are normally distributed. There are formal ways in which to test for normality of error distributions if small samples make that assumption necessary.

Next, if two or more distributions are normal, then they only need a common population mean and a common variance to be identical. Mathematically, all normal distributions have the same equation, and the only parameters in that equation are μ and σ^2 (the mean and the variance). If the null hypothesis of no treatment effects is true, then all the means come from sampling distributions that are centered around the population mean, μ. That is, all of the means of the sampling distributions will equal μ, and this takes care of the common mean requirement.

The only way in which to satisfy the common variance requirement would be for all populations to have the same variance *and* for all samples to be the same size. The property of equal population variances is called *homoscedasticity* in the formal jargon of statistics.

Unless we have prior information about the population variances, we will have to assume homoscedasticity or test for it. There are ways in which to test such an assumption. For now, simply recognize that a crucial part of ANOVA is the assumption that the populations from which the samples came have equal variances. That still leaves us with the problem of equal sample sizes. For the stooge experiment data, each treatment had 12 cases. It is not uncommon, however, to have samples of different sizes, and we want an approach that is not restricted to special cases.

The three criteria just discussed are summarized in the following box. This may seem a long way from analyzing our data, but what we have done is set up the logic for a precise calculation of the chance that the group means could differ as much as they do purely because of random sampling variations.

To Summarize So Far:

1. We need to have either
   (a) a normally distributed error distributions or
   (b) large enough samples
   in order to assume normality.

2. We need to assume homoscedasticity:

   $$\sigma_1^2 = \sigma_2^2 = \ldots = \sigma_k^2 = \sigma^2,$$

   that is, that the populations have a common variance.

3. We will assume initially that the null hypothesis,

   $$\mu_1 = \mu_2 = \ldots = \mu_k = \mu,$$

   is true.

With these three conditions met, we can use the variability of the sample means to estimate the variance of the common sampling distribution.

Two Estimates of Variance

Now let's put the pieces together for calculating ANOVA. First, look at how much the values of Y vary *within* the samples. We have assumed normally distributed error terms for each of the populations and that the mean error is zero. Homoscedasticity says that all populations have the same variance. All observed error terms, $e_{i,j}$, come from normal distributions with the same mean, zero, and the same variance, σ_y^2. Statistically, they are from the same population, and so we combine all the observed error terms into one "pooled" estimate of that common population variance. Pooling simply refers to using the information from all cases in all groups for a single estimate. When all the squared deviations of cases from their respective group means have been added, the sum is divided by the appropriate degrees of freedom for one estimate of σ_y^2. Call this the *within-groups* estimate of variance.

As discussed previously, if the null hypothesis is true and the assumptions of normality and homoscedasticity are reasonable, then we can also use how much the means vary around the overall mean to estimate σ_y^2. That is accomplished by estimating the variance of the sampling distribution of the sample means, weighted by sample size. Call this the *between-means* estimate of variance.

We now have two ways in which to estimate the same variance, σ_y^2, under the null hypothesis that there were no treatment effects if the assumptions of normality and homoscedasticity are valid. Because these are estimates of the same variance, they should agree. If the estimates disagree too much and we have reason to be confident in the underlying assumptions, then the only weak link in the chain of logic is having assumed that the null hypothesis is true. Therefore, if the two estimates of variance *dis*agree by too much, we can conclude that the sample means differ by too much to be attributable to chance. By implication, the population means really do differ. The logical conclusion is that the null hypothesis is wrong and the treatments did indeed have an effect. That is the same as saying that the β_j values do differ from each other.

Stop a moment to reflect on the reasoning just outlined. This argument is the statistician's equivalent of the logician's *reductio ad adsurdum* (reduction to an absurdity). If we make a set of reasonable assumptions and find that the logical implication of those assumptions is absurd (extremely unlikely) in light of our evidence, then either (a) our evidence has to be wrong, (b) our deductions are faulty, or (c) our assumptions are called wrong.

As careful researchers we should be able to trust our evidence, and as careful statisticians we can determine the reasonableness of the normality and homoscedasticity assumptions. We know from mathematical statisticians that the deductive logic is correct as long as these assumptions are valid. If all that holds and the results are absurdly unlikely under the hypothesis of no group effects, then our only recourse, using the logic of formal hypothesis testing, is to reject that hypothesis in favor of the alternative hypothesis that the population means do differ—that the treatments did indeed have differential effects. There is always the possibility of making a Type I error using this logic, but at least we can decide in advance what chance we are willing to take of making such an error. That chance is α, which we set in advance.

Calculating Sums of Squares

Any variance estimate has two parts. The numerator always is a sum of squares; the denominator is the appropriate degrees of freedom. For the estimate based on variation among the sample means, we need to calculate the deviation of each group mean from the overall mean of all the cases, square that deviation, weight it by sample size, and add over all groups. This will give us the *between-means sum of squares*. For convenience, designate this sum as SS_B.

In the example of Exhibit 3.1, there are four sample means: .3867, −.0483, .4292, and −.3442. The overall mean is .0425. Subtract the overall mean from each group mean, square that difference, and then weight (i.e., multiply) by the number of cases in that group. Because we only want the sum of squares, SS_B, for now, we will ignore degrees of freedom. Calculations for SS_B are

$$12 \, (.3867 - .0425)^2$$
$$+ \, 12 \, (-.0483 - .0425)^2$$
$$+ \, 12 \, (.4292 - .0425)^2$$
$$+ \, 12 \, (-.3442 - .0425)^2 = 4.9162.$$

Actually, if you use these figures, then you should get 4.9169, but the fourth decimal place is in error because of rounding the group means. We will use the more accurate 4.9162.

It is typical to use a simpler computational form for SS_B. The definitional form just used parallels that for the numerator of any variance:

$$SS_B = \sum_j n_j \, (\overline{Y}_{.j} - \overline{Y}_{..})^2 . \tag{3.5}$$

Remember that Σ (capital sigma) means to add what follows, the subscript j says to do it for each group, and, of course, you square what is in the parentheses first. Therefore, Equation 3.5 says the following:

> For each group, (a) subtract the overall mean from the group mean, (b) square that difference, and (c) multiply by the number of cases in the group. Then (d) add these weighted, squared differences over all groups.

Computationally, if you have to do the work yourself rather than having a computer program do it, it is easier to work with sums than with means. Equation 3.6, to follow, gives exactly the same answer as does Equation 3.5, but it is much easier to use, especially if you have a lot of data and your group means are not nice even numbers. Appendix A contains a demonstration of the algebraic equivalence of the two formulas. Each step in the demonstration is explained. Work through it so that you can become more comfortable with equations of this type. The rest of the book contains quite a few of them.

$$SS_B = \sum_j \frac{\left(\sum_i Y_{ij}\right)^2}{n_j} - \frac{\left(\sum_j \sum_i Y_{ij}\right)^2}{\sum_j n_j}. \tag{3.6}$$

Equation 3.6 looks pretty messy, but the computations it specifies are quite simple. The first term says the following: For each group, (a) add up all the values of Y in that group, (b) square that group total, and (c) divide the squared total by the size of the group. Then (d) add these results over all the groups. If you follow the subscripts carefully and work inside the brackets first, then that set of steps should become apparent. The second term says to (a) add up all values of Y for all cases in all groups, (b) square this grand total, and (c) divide it by the total number of cases in all groups. Either Equation 3.5 or Equation 3.6 will give you SS_B, the between-means sum of squares. Try working through the data in Exhibit 3.1 using Equation 3.6 to see whether you can get the same answer obtained earlier: $SS_B = 5.4538 - .5376 = 4.9162$.

To calculate the within-groups sum of squares, or SS_W, you need to do the following: (a) take each value of Y, (b) subtract the mean for the group which that case is in, (c) square the result, and (d) add these squared deviations over all cases in all groups. In equation form, that looks like

$$SS_W = \sum_j \sum_i (Y_{ij} - \bar{Y}_j)^2 . \qquad (3.7)$$

Equation 3.7 is a definitional equation for SS_W, just like Equation 3.5 is the definitional formula for SS_B. It, too, has a more convenient computational form if there are a lot of data and the overall mean is not a nice even number.

The computational equivalent of Equation 3.7 is shown in Equation 3.8, to follow. Appendix B has a demonstration of the equivalence of the two formulas, with a complete explanation of each of the steps. Again, you should try to work through the algebra for familiarity and practice.

$$SS_W = \sum_j \sum_i Y_{ij}^2 - \sum_j \frac{\left(\sum_i Y_{ij}\right)^2}{n_j} . \qquad (3.8)$$

The first term of Equation 3.8 says to square each value of Y for all cases in all groups and add up those squared values. The second term in Equation 3.8 is exactly the same as the first term in Equation 3.6, and its interpretation is the same as it was then. Using the computational form, calculations for SS_W with the data in Exhibit 3.1 are as follows:

$1.50^2 + 1.25^2 + 1.00^2 + .75^2 + .39^2 + 0^2 + 0^2 + 0^2 + 0^2 + 0^2 + 0^2 + -.25^2$
$+ 1.00^2 + .50^2 + .50^2 + 0^2 + 0^2 + 0^2 + 0^2 + 0^2 + -.08^2 + -.50^2 + -1.00^2$
$+ -1.00^2 + 1.50^2 + 1.25^2 + 1.00^2 + 1.00^2 + .50^2 + 0^2 + 0^2 + 0^2 + 0^2 + 0^2$
$+ 0^2 + -.10^2 + .50^2 + .27^2 + 0^2 + 0^2 + 0^2 + 0^2 + -.34^2 + -.40^2 + -.89^2 + -1.00^2$
$+ -1.00^2 + -1.27^2 = 20.4220.$

$SS_W = 20.4220 - 5.4538 = 14.9682.$

As with the between and within sums of squares, the total sum of squares, SS_T, can be obtained either by a definitional equation or a computational one. Each is shown in Equation 3.9. The second line is the computational version. You can see that the first term of that version is the same as the first term for SS_W in Equation 3.8. Similarly, the second term is the same as the second term for SS_B in Equation 3.6. Therefore, $SS_T = 20.4220 - .5376 = 19.8844.$

$$SS_T = \sum_i \sum_j (Y_{ij} - \bar{Y}_j)^2 = \sum_j \sum_i Y_{ij}^2 - \frac{\left(\sum_j \sum_i Y_{ij}\right)^2}{\sum_j n_j}. \quad (3.9)$$

It should be evident, therefore, that $SS_T = SS_B + SS_W$. In words, the total sum of squares has been divided into two separate sums: the between and the within. These are independent sums if the errors that make up SS_W are truly random.

Degrees of Freedom

We finally have two computational formulas for the sums of squares needed to calculate an ANOVA. Remember, however, that these are the numerators for estimates of variance. Any variance estimate needs a sum of squares divided by its appropriate degrees of freedom. In general, the degrees of freedom will equal the number of squared deviations entered into the sum, minus 1 for each sample estimate of a population parameter that we have to use in our calculations. For the between-means estimate of variance, we squared the deviation of each group mean from the grand mean and then added those squared terms. Theoretically, the deviations should be around μ, but because we do not know the value of μ, we use the grand mean calculated from sample data as an estimate of μ. There will be as many degrees of freedom as there are groups, minus 1 for this estimate of μ. Therefore, for J groups,

$$df_B = J - 1.$$

Obviously, for the data in Exhibit 3.1, $df_B = 4 - 1 = 3$.

Similarly, for the within-groups estimate of variance, we squared each case's deviation around its group mean and then added these squared deviations over all cases. For this computation, the deviations would be calculated around μ_j for each group j if we knew the μ_j values. Because we do not know those values, we again have had to use the sample means as estimates of the μ_j values. With a total of n cases, there are n squared deviations entered into the sum. With J groups, we lose J df by estimating the μ_j. Consequently,

$$df_W = n - J.$$

For the data in Exhibit 3.1, $n = 48$ and $J = 4$, and so $df_W = 48 - 4 = 44$.

Exhibit 3.3

Analysis of Variance Table

Source	SS	df	MS	F
Between	4.9162	3	1.6387	4.8171**
Within	14.9682	44	0.3402	
Total	19.8844	47		

**Significant at $\alpha = .01$.

Calculating One-Way ANOVA

Finally, we are ready. The complete ANOVA table for a one-way analysis looks like Exhibit 3.3. The column headings may differ somewhat from one text to another, but the information needed is the same. The first column, for source, indicates whether the data are from the between, within, or total computations. The next column, SS, reports the three sums of squares from those different sources. We calculated each of those values previously, and so all that is necessary is to enter them on the appropriate line. Be certain that $SS_T = SS_B + SS_W$. The third column shows appropriate degrees of freedom, which we also calculated previously.

Remember that what we have been doing is calculating two independent estimates of σ_Y^2. Because a variance estimate consists of a sum of squares divided by appropriate degrees of freedom, the next step is to do the dividing and enter the answers in the column headed MS, short for *mean square*. It is not necessary to do the calculations for the "total" row because we are interested only in comparing the between and within estimates. The final step for setting up the ANOVA table is to calculate F, which is a simple ratio: $F = MS_B / MS_W$. As you can see in Exhibit 3.3, $F = 4.8171$.

Now comes the question of what to do with F once we have it calculated. First, turn to the F table in the back of the book. Note that the table is grouped into pairs of rows for each entry in the *df* column: the first row is for $\alpha = .05$; the second row is for $\alpha = .01$. One of the problems with F, compared to simpler distributions, is that it would require many, many pages to accommodate a wide range of α levels, and so typically only the most commonly desired levels of α are included.

The value of α should be established before gathering data because the chance one is willing to take of making a Type I error should be independent of the research findings. That is, α should depend on theoretical or practical implications of the work being done. Assume that, as is common, we had established $\alpha = .05$, and so we will start with the $\alpha = .05$ part of the F table. Notice that there are different columns for the degrees of freedom associated with the numerator estimate of variance and different rows for the df associated with the denominator estimate of variance. Because the numerator estimate is MS_B, we want the column headed 3 because $df_B = 3$. The denominator estimate is MS_W, and $df_W = 44$. Therefore, we look for a row headed 44. Unfortunately, there is no column headed 44. Now what? The thing to do when you cannot find the right degrees of freedom in the table is to choose the next *smallest* degrees of freedom. In this case, we want the row headed 40. To choose a larger degrees of freedom row would in effect increase α.

The value of F you want is in the cell defined by the column and the row just chosen; in this case, the column for $df = 3$ and the row for $df = 40$. The value of F in that cell is 2.84. What that value indicates is that 95% of the time you can expect values of F from 0 to 2.84 if the null hypothesis is true. In other words, even if the population means are identical, 95% of the time you ran such experiments you could get random variation in group means that would generate an F ratio as large as 2.84. Larger values of F would occur less often than 5% of the time if the null hypothesis were true. Following the formal test logic discussed in Chapter 2, if the calculated F exceeds the table value of F, then reject the null hypothesis in favor of its alternative.

Our calculated value of F is 4.8171, which clearly is larger than the table value of 2.84. We reject the null hypothesis with 95% confidence that the observed treatment means differ more than would be expected if the population means were all the same. The consequence is to conclude that the population means really do differ: The treatments did have differential effect.

As noted in Chapter 2, some researchers simply report the level of significance of the results and do not formally test a hypothesis. Because the calculated F is considerably larger than the table value of F for $\alpha = .05$, we could go to the $\alpha = .01$ portion of the table. Again using the column headed 3 and the row headed 40, the table value of F is 4.31. Once again, the calculated value of F is greater than the table value, and so it would be reasonable to state that the results are significant at the $\alpha = .01$ level. Usually, a significant result at the .05 level is shown with one asterisk, and a significant result at the

.01 level is shown with two asterisks. As you can see in Exhibit 3.3, there are two asterisks after the F value.

Doing Calculations by Hand

A simple way in which to keep track of the calculations, if you are doing them by hand and the number of cases per treatment is not too large, is to construct a table such as that shown in Exhibit 3.4. As in Exhibit 3.1, each column in the table represents one treatment, and the entries are the values of Y for each of the 12 subjects in that treatment. There are three extra rows added to the table: one for the sum of the values of Y in each group, headed ΣY, one for the sum of squared values of Y in each group, headed ΣY^2, and one for the number of cases in the group, n. These are the pieces of information you need for the calculation formulas shown earlier in Equations 3.6 and 3.8. If you are using a calculator, then just add up the values of Y for each column and record them in the ΣY row for that column. Similarly, square each value of Y and add those squares for each group. That value goes in the ΣY^2 row for that group. Entering the values of n does not require any calculating, of course, but it keeps all the data you need together. Then you can simply fill in the appropriate pieces of each formula and calculate the needed sums of squares and degrees of freedom for the ANOVA table. A table like that in Exhibit 3.4 is very cumbersome if there is a large number of cases.

Doing ANOVA With SPSS

Calculations for ANOVA were pretty easy with the stooge data, but they can be terribly tedious with large samples or multiple factors or covariates. Further, you risk making calculation errors if you do the work by hand. Instead, you could use any of several computer statistical packages. Because it is so widely used, SPSS will be illustrated here. The two main versions of SPSS are SPSS for Windows and SPSS-PC. Illustrations for the latter are shown here, although there are only minor differences between the versions. To call up SPSS-PC, just type *SPSSPC* and then create the command file shown in Exhibit 3.5.

SPSS-PC allows you to work interactively in setting up a file to run your analysis, or you can type your own command file directly,

Exhibit 3.4

Calculations for ANOVA

	Group 1 (neat-con)	Group 2 (neat-hes)	Group 3 (sloppy-con)	Group 4 (sloppy-hes)
	1.50	1.00	1.50	.50
	1.25	.50	1.25	.27
	1.00	.50	1.00	0
	.75	0	1.00	0
	.39	0	.50	0
	0	0	0	0
	0	0	0	−.34
	0	0	0	−.40
	0	−.08	0	−.89
	0	−.50	0	−1.00
	0	−1.00	0	−1.00
	−.25	−1.00	−.10	−1.27
ΣY	4.64	−.58	5.15	−4.13
ΣY^2	5.5896	3.7564	6.0725	5.0035
n	12	12	12	12

as was done with the file in Exhibit 3.5. You can bypass the interactive menu by holding down the <Alt> key and typing *e*, which allows direct editing of your command file. Then you can type commands and data directly. Alternatively, you can use the SPSS menu system for selecting the commands you need. Unless you tell SPSS to read external files, however, you still need to type in your labels and data.

The commands in Exhibit 3.5 are quite simple. The first line starts with the DATA LIST command, which tells SPSS to expect information needed to set up a data file. The term FREE specifies a free-field format for reading data, and the two short labels, ROLE and RATING, are for the independent and dependent variables in the data set, respectively. These labels cannot exceed eight characters each, and so the next two lines, VAR LABELS, provide longer versions of the labels for eventual printout. Note, by the way, that there are single quotes around the long versions of the labels. Also, you must end each separate command with a period.

VALUE LABELS gives SPSS names to use in the printout for each value of ROLE. There are four roles. Which role a subject was is the first entry on the data lines below. (ROLE was listed as the first variable in the DATA LIST line.) Again, there are single quotes around the labels.

Exhibit 3.5

SPSS Command File for One-Way ANOVA

```
DATA LIST FREE / ROLE RATING.
VAR LABELS  ROLE 'STOOGE ROLE' RATING 'RATING OF STOOGE PERFORMANCE'.
VALUE LABELS ROLE  1 'NEAT-CON'  2 'NEAT-HES' 3 'SLOP-CON' 4 'SLOP-HES'.
TITLE STOOGE EXPERIMENTS: ONE-WAY ANOVA.
BEGIN DATA
1  1.50
1  1.25
1  1.00
1  0.75
1  0.39
1  0
1  0
1  0
1  0
1  0
1  0
1 -.25
2  1.00
2  0.50
2  0.50
2  0
2  0
2  0
2  0
2  0
2 -0.08
2 -0.50
2 -1.00
2 -1.00
3  1.50
3  1.25
3  1.00
3  1.00
3  0.50
3  0
3  0
3  0
3  0
3  0
3  0
3 -0.10
4  0.50
4  0.27
4  0
4  0
4  0
4  0
4 -0.34
4 -0.40
4 -0.89
4 -1.00
4 -1.00
4 -1.27
END DATA.
ONEWAY RATING BY ROLE (1,4)
/OPTIONS=6
/STATISTICS=1.
```

You do not need a title line, but it helps remind you of what you ran. The title does not have to be in parentheses. The BEGIN DATA and END DATA lines bracket the data. If you had a separate data file, then you could avoid entering the data this way and simply call for that file to be read. Finally, the last three commands tell SPSS to run a one-way ANOVA analyzing RATING by ROLE. The (1,4) after ROLE tells SPSS to use values of ROLE from 1 to 4. Note that there is no period here because the command continues with OPTIONS=6, which calls for using the group labels provided earlier. It will use up to eight characters; this is why the labels were not typed out in full. The STATISTICS=1 line calls for group descriptive statistics, which can help in interpreting the results.

When the entire command set is typed in, all that is needed is to put the cursor at the head of the command file, press <F10> and then <Enter>. SPSS will display calculations on the screen and also write files you can save for permanent records of your run. Exhibits 3.6 and 3.7 show relevant portions of the SPSS output produced by the commands in Exhibit 3.5. The only differences between Exhibit 3.6 and Exhibit 3.3, our earlier F table, is that SPSS lists the df column before the SS column and also provides a specific probability estimate rather than simply asterisks (or "n.s.") to indicate significance.

The calculated probability, which you can see is only .0055, is the chance that we would have observed as much variance among the sample means as we did if there was no difference between the means of the populations from which the samples were drawn. Obviously, such a small probability prompts us to reject the null hypothesis that $\mu_1 = \mu_2 = \mu_3 = \mu_4$. The results of this SPSS run exactly match our earlier calculations.

Exhibit 3.7 provides data for the individual groups; it shows group means, standard deviations, standard errors for the means, and 95% confidence limits for estimates of the values of μ_j. The lower part of Exhibit 3.7 gives the lowest and highest observed scores for each of the groups. All of the information in Exhibit 3.7 was obtained by the command STATISTICS=1.

Note that if you take almost all possible pairs of groups (e.g., NEAT-CON vs. NEAT-HES [neat-confident vs. neat-hesitant]), their confidence limits overlap. In fact, the only pair of groups for which that is not true is SLOP-CON versus SLOP-HES (sloppy-confident vs. sloppy-hesitant). Had we run a one-way ANOVA using only the data for the two sloppy treatments, we would have had a significant F. Running any of the other pairs of treatments by themselves would

Exhibit 3.6

SPSS Printout: Basic ANOVA Table

Analysis of Variance

Source	D.F.	Sum of Squares	Mean Squares	F Ratio	F Prob.
Between Groups	3	4.9162	1.6387	4.8171	.0055
Within Groups	44	14.9682	.3402		
Total	47	19.8844			

Exhibit 3.7

SPSS Printout: Group Data

Group	Count	Mean	Standard Deviation	Standard Error	95 Pct Conf Int for Mean		
NEAT-CON	12	.3867	.5874	.1696	.0134	To	.7599
NEAT-HES	12	-.0483	.5822	.1681	-.4182	To	.3216
SLOP-CON	12	.4292	.5926	.1711	.0527	To	.6057
SLOP-HES	12	-.3442	.5707	.1647	-.7067	To	.0184
Total	48	.1058	.6504	.0939	.0134	To	.2947

Group	Minimum	Maximum
NEAT-CON	-.2500	1.5000
NEAT-HES	-1.0000	1.0000
SLOP-CON	-.1000	1.5000
SLOP-HES	-1.2700	.5000
Total	-1.2700	1.5000

have resulted in a different conclusion. The point is that ANOVA has tested whether the four group means differ enough to warrant the conclusion, given our chosen level of α, that the population means differ. That does not imply that *all* values of μ will be different. It only means that at least one value of μ is different from the others so that the statement that all are equal is false. There are proper ways in which to test hypotheses about individual pairs of population means. They are discussed in Chapter 4.

Summary

A lot has been done in this chapter. We began with some basic definitions and notation, followed by a formal model of effects in a one-way ANOVA. That model has three explicit components: the overall population mean, specific group effects, and random error. Next we returned to the notion of a sampling distribution, which enables an estimate of the *population* variance based on the variance of the sample means *if* the null hypothesis that the population means are equal is true. That is how the between estimate of σ_y^2 is developed. Separately, if the assumption of homoscedasticity is warranted, then it is possible to pool the within-sample variation to generate the within estimate of σ_y^2.

The logic that leads to these two ways in which to estimate what should be the same variance is absolutely crucial to your understanding of what ANOVA is all about. If the null hypothesis is true and the assumptions all are valid, then the variation among the separate sample (or group) means should be no more than would be expected by chance. We can use their variation to estimate the (assumed) common population variance and then compare that estimate with one based on pooling the within-sample variation of cases around their sample means.

Following the logic of a formal hypothesis test, if these two estimates agree, as evidenced by a small F ratio, then the sample means do not differ enough to reject the null hypothesis that the population means are the same. Remember, however, that there always is the chance of a Type II error: accepting a false hypothesis. If the calculated F is larger than the table values for α, df_B, and df_W, then the sample results are too unlikely under the hypothesis that the population means are the same. *Too unlikely* means that there is less chance than α that the sample results would have occurred if the null hypothesis were true.

Now the sample results are "real." Therefore, if F is significant, the assumptions all are reasonable, and the calculations are correct, then the test logic says that the null hypothesis itself would seem to be in error, so we reject it. The populations really do differ. It is important to keep in mind, however, that there is a difference between the certainty of a purely logical model and the uncertainty of statistical inference. The pure logic says that if results are impossible under stated premises, and if those results are not suspect, then one or more of the premises must be in error. The statistical logic says that if the chance that observed results would occur under the null hypothesis is too small, then we will reject that hypothesis. This is not a sure bet; it is subject to Type I error. At least we can specify via α the chance we are willing to take of making such an error.

As stated at the outset of this chapter, one-way ANOVA is the simplest form of analysis of variance. There is only one source of systematic variation formally included in our model: the different experimental conditions. However, we might well ask whether one or more other factors could affect our results. Do women react to the experiment differently from men? What about older people versus younger people, or different racial or ethnic groups? If we turned to social psychological theory about factors that influence person perception or interpersonal behavior, then we could find numerous variables that might well affect evaluations of contributions to group process. A larger set of explanatory variables would necessitate a more complicated experimental design. Chapter 5 extends ANOVA to cover multiple factors at the same time so that we can sort out how much of our results is due to each of those factors while controlling for the other factors.

Several other texts provide helpful presentations of ANOVA. You might find it useful to read Collyer and Enns (1986), Edwards (1979), and Iversen and Norpoth (1987).

APPENDIX A

Demonstration of the Equivalence of Definitional
and Computational Equations for SS_B

The following derivation is provided in part so that you understand the equivalence of the definitional and computation forms
and in part to help you get used to the notation and working with
the equations. Even if you are not comfortable with algebra, try to
work through the derivation. Each step is explained to help you
understand.

Let's start with Equation 3.5, which was

$$SS_B = \sum_j n_j (\overline{Y}_{.j} - \overline{Y}_{..})^2 .$$

First, write out the squared difference (called *expanding* the square).
For a squared difference like that in Equation 3.5, the expansion will
have the first term squared, minus two times the product of the
terms, plus the square of the last term:

$$SS_B = \sum_j n_j (\overline{Y}_{.j}^2 - 2\overline{Y}_{.j}\overline{Y}_{..} + \overline{Y}_{..}^2) .$$

Next, distribute the n_j from outside the parentheses to each term
inside and also distribute the summations sign, Σ:

$$SS_B = \sum_j n_j \overline{Y}_{.j}^2 - 2\overline{Y}_{..} \sum_j n_j \overline{Y}_{.j}^2 + \overline{Y}_{..}^2 \sum_j n_j .$$

Of course, the grand mean is constant for all groups, and so we can
factor that constant out of the group-level summation. Remember for
the mean of group j to add the values of Y over all cases in group j
and divide by n_j. For the grand mean, add the values of Y over all
cases in the entire sample (over all groups and all cases in those
groups) and divide by the total number of all cases in all groups, n.

Let's examine each of the three terms separately. The first term
is simple. It can be reexpressed as

$$\sum_j n_j \left(\frac{\sum_i Y_{ij}}{n_j} \right)^2 ,$$

but the n_j term in front of the brackets will cancel out the square of that term in the denominator inside the brackets. Therefore, the first term becomes

$$\sum_j \frac{\left(\sum_i Y_{ij}\right)^2}{n_j}.$$

The second term can be rewritten, again substituting sums and ns for means, as

$$2 \left(\frac{\sum_j \sum_i Y_{ij}}{n}\right)^2 \sum_j n_j \left(\frac{\sum_i Y_{ij}}{n_j}\right)^2.$$

The n_j terms cancel out each other, allowing the right portion of the expression to become $\sum\sum Y_{ij}$, which is exactly like the first part. Therefore, the entire second term becomes

$$-2 \frac{\left(\sum_j \sum_i Y_{ij}\right)^2}{n}.$$

For the last term, it should be apparent that $\sum n_j = n$ because the size of the total sample is just the sum of the sizes of the group samples. The last term, then, becomes

$$n \left(\frac{\sum_j \sum_i Y_{ij}}{n}\right)^2 = \frac{\left(\sum_j \sum_i Y_{ij}\right)^2}{n_j}.$$

Now, the second term is -2 times the square of the sum of all cases, divided by n, and the last term is 1 times that same amount, and so the last term cancels out the -2 of the second term, leaving only -1 of that term. The entire expression for SS_B reduces to Equation 3.6, shown as follows, and we have proved the equivalence of the definitional and computational forms:

$$SS_B = \sum_j \frac{\left(\sum_i Y_{ij}\right)^2}{n_j} - \frac{\left(\sum_j \sum_i Y_{ij}\right)^2}{n}.$$

APPENDIX B

Demonstration of the Equivalence of Definitional
and Computational Equations for SS_W

We begin with Equation 3.7, the definitional form for the within-groups sum of squares.

$$SS_W = \sum_j \sum_i (Y_{ij} - \overline{Y}_{.j})^2 .$$

If we expand the squared term in the parentheses, we get

$$SS_W = \sum_j \sum_i (Y_{ij}^2 - 2 Y_{ij} \overline{Y}_{.j}) + \overline{Y}_{.j}^2 .$$

Distributing the summation, as was done in Appendix A for SS_B, results in

$$SS_W = \sum_j \sum_i Y_{ij}^2 - 2 \sum_j \left(\overline{Y}_{ij} \sum_i Y_{ij} \right) + \sum_j \sum_i \overline{Y}_{.j}^2 .$$

Let's leave the first term alone because we cannot do anything further with it. Substituting $\Sigma Y_{ij}/n_j$ for the group mean in the second term gives us

$$-2 \sum_j \left(\frac{\sum_i Y_{ij}}{n_j} \right) \sum_i Y_{ij} ,$$

but of course the same sum of Y scores appears both inside and outside the brackets, so the term can be reexpressed as

$$-2 \sum_j \frac{\left(\sum_i Y_{ij} \right)^2}{n_j} .$$

We will leave that term as it is for now.

Finally, in the last term for SS_W, each group mean is constant for all cases in that group, and so it can be factored out of the Σ_i portion of the term. The term can then be reexpressed as

$$\sum_j \left(\overline{Y}_{.j}^2 \sum_i \right) .$$

It looks a bit strange to have Σ_i by itself. If you imagine a 1 after the summation sign, then you can see that Σ_i means to add a 1 for each case in the group, and this amounts to counting the number of cases in the group. Therefore, Σ_i for group j equals n_j. Using that fact and again substituting a sum over group size for the group mean, we can see that the last term becomes

$$\sum_j \frac{\left(\sum_i Y_{ij}\right)^2}{n_j}.$$

Parallel to the proof for SS_B, the second term is -2 times this third term. Therefore, the final expression for SS_W becomes Equation 3.8, which is the computational form for SS_W, and again we have proved the equivalence of the definitional and computational forms.

$$SS_W = \sum_j \sum_i Y_{ij}^2 - \sum_j \frac{\left(\sum_i Y_{ij}\right)^2}{n_j}.$$

4 Contrasts and Effects: Comparing Treatments

Our formal models have used μ and β_j to refer to average effects in the population under study. The overall average of subjects in the population is μ, and β_j is how much difference treatment j makes, or the difference between the overall population average and the population average for subjects experiencing treatment j. The F test for one-way AVOVA simply asks, "What is the chance that the variance of the treatment means is this large if the null hypothesis is true?" That is the same as asking whether the β_j values differ enough to reject a purely random model at the chosen α level. When we used ANOVA to test a "no-effects" hypothesis on the stooge data, the F was significant and we could conclude that, at the $\alpha = .05$ level of significance, the different stooge roles had differential effects on how the stooges were evaluated.

What we do not know from the ANOVA F test is whether *all* of the treatments differ from each other. It is possible that one particular treatment makes a big difference, whereas the others do not have much effect. Another possible pattern would be that two treatments have similar effects that are different from the other two treatments, which also have similar effects. In fact, there could be a number of different patterns that would generate a significant F without having all treatments different from each other. It is useful, therefore, to have a statistical logic for asking whether specific subsets of treatments differ from each other. Such comparisons of specific subsets of treatments are called *contrasts*.

Defining Contrasts

There are two questions to consider in deciding how to proceed with testing specific treatment differences. One is whether there are theoretical reasons for predicting particular differences among the treatments in advance of looking at the actual data. Then the tests to be developed are theory driven and do not depend on having spotted results that happen to look good. When data already have been tabulated before such tests are defined, it is too easy to focus on large differences that may have been accidents of random sampling. The second question concerns whether the contrasts are statistically independent so that the results of one test do not have implications for any of the other tests.

A Priori Versus A Posteriori Tests

Hypotheses that have been specified prior to looking at the data are called *a priori* hypotheses. Those that are defined after the data are known are *a posteriori* tests. It certainly is not "wrong" to conduct a posteriori tests, but there are two major reasons for conducting a priori tests. First, because they are theory driven, they have maximal implication for the theory underlying the research. A posteriori tests, on the other hand, are ad hoc in character and may be minimally relevant to basic theoretical questions. Consequently, if it is possible to specify meaningful contrasts a priori, then the information gained will be more productive theoretically.

The second advantage is that, in general, a priori tests preserve statistical confidence, whereas a posteriori tests require major adjustments in α. Suppose you conduct an experiment, calculate the results, look over the various differences between pairs of group means, and see one that looks particularly large. If you then test that one difference using your original value of α, you already have biased the test in your favor. There always is some nonzero chance of getting a large difference when the null hypothesis is true. At the .05 level, you would expect, on the average, one significant difference every 20 tests when no differences existed among the populations. By simply seizing on obvious differences rather than performing theoretically driven tests, you greatly increase the chance of finding significance when the null hypothesis is true.

Even if you are not seizing on obvious differences, the more ad hoc tests you conduct, the more chance there is of obtaining significant results by chance. Either confidence will be eroded or you will have to adjust α to a much smaller amount to ensure that all of the tests are meaningful at the original level of confidence.

Simply "dredging" data, either by testing everything or by looking around for any possible effect that reaches an arbitrary level of significance, greatly increases the chance of a Type I error beyond the specified α level. Although there are appropriate procedures for conducting a posteriori tests, only a priori tests will be considered here. More advanced discussions of probabilities and error rates than there is space for here will be necessary for an adequate treatment of a posteriori procedures.

Orthogonal Contrasts

How do you decide what contrasts to test? At first it may seem like a good idea to conduct t tests for all possible contrasts. However, a full set of possible contrasts would be interdependent and thus correlated. If group 1 is significantly greater than group 2, and if group 2 is significantly greater than group 3, then there is a greater chance that group 1 is significantly greater than group 3 than would be the case if the previous contrasts were not significant. Orthogonal tests are needed.

A set of contrasts are said to be *orthogonal* if they are uncorrelated. The tests are correlated if the results of one test have implications for one or more of the other tests. Whenever there are such mutual implications of a set of possible contrasts, separately testing all of those differences at any preset level of α would erode our confidence in any of the tests. Conducting all those *inter*dependent tests at the .05 level of α would result in a much larger probability of making a Type I error.

Exhibit 4.1 shows the full set of possible contrasts for a four-group experiment. With four treatments, there are 6 different treatment pairs that could be contrasted, plus 3 possible contrasts combining 2 treatments versus 2 other treatments, plus 4 possible contrasts of 1 treatment versus the combined other 3. That makes 13 conceivable contrasts.

Unfortunately, there are only $J - 1$ orthogonal contrasts that can be created for J groups or treatments, and that will be fewer than the total number of contrasts that logically could be constructed. Again, for four treatments, there can be only $4 - 1 = 3$ orthogonal contrasts.

Suppose we tested the following null hypotheses:

$H_a: \mu_1 = (\mu_2 + \mu_3 + \mu_4)/3$ Treatment 1 is no different from the average of the other three treatments.

Exhibit 4.1

All Possible Contrasts for a Four-Group Experiment

Type of Contrast	Possible Contrasts
Comparing one treatment versus another, while ignoring the remaining two treatments	Gp 1 vs Gp 2 Gp 1 vs Gp 3 Gp 1 vs Gp 4 Gp 2 vs Gp 3 Gp 2 vs Gp 4 Gp 3 vs Gp 4
Comparing one pair of treatments versus the other pair of treatments	(Gp 1 + Gp 2) vs (Gp 3 + Gp 4) (Gp 1 + Gp 3) vs (Gp 2 + Gp 4) (Gp 1 + Gp 4) vs (Gp 2 + Gp 3)
Comparing one treatment versus the other three treatments	Gp 1 vs (Gp 2 + Gp 3 + Gp 4) Gp 2 vs (Gp 1 + Gp 3 + Gp 4) Gp 3 vs (Gp 1 + Gp 2 + Gp 4) Gp 4 vs (Gp 1 + Gp 2 + Gp 3)

H_b: $\mu_2 = (\mu_3 + \mu_4)/2$ Treatment 2 is no different from the average of treatments 3 and 4.

H_c: $\mu_3 = \mu_4$ Treatment 3 is no different from treatment 4.

Any of these hypotheses could be false without having implications for independently testing the other hypotheses in the set. However, you cannot state any fourth hypothesis about these four population means that is not in part implied by at least one of the three hypotheses already stated.

There are many sets of possible independent hypotheses; these three are just one possible set. Moreover, just stating three hypotheses does not automatically make them independent. As noted, *orthogonal* means statistically independent; orthogonal contrasts are tests that are uncorrelated with each other. Incidentally, do not confuse the term *orthogonal* with *a priori*. One says the tests are independent; the other says they are based on prior theoretical considerations.

Consider possible hypotheses about the relative effectiveness of the four stooge roles. Based on research about person perception, we could hypothesize that the two confident roles will generate different ratings than will the two hesitant roles. Based on knowledge of the specific campus culture at the time of the experiments, we might hypothesize that the sloppy-confident role will generate different ratings than will the neat-confident role. Finally, if we had reason to believe that the effects of hesitance would overshadow any appearance factor, we could hypothesize that the two hesitant roles will be indistinguishable in their effects. These three hypotheses are both a priori and orthogonal. Most important, they are based on reasonable theoretical predictions.

These predictions constitute substantive hypotheses, but re-member that ANOVA tests only formal null (no effect) hypotheses. We need to restate our three hypotheses in formal null form. Also, you might have realized that we could have made stronger predic-tions than just "no difference" for the first two hypotheses because we would expect the confident role to be evaluated higher than the hesitant role and, in the campus culture context of that time, we might expect the sloppy role to outshine the neat role. For now, however, we will concentrate on nondirectional null hypotheses.

Stated verbally, the first null hypothesis is that the combined mean for treatments 1 and 3 (the confident treatments) equals the combined mean for treatments 2 and 4 (the hesitant treatments). Formally, the hypothesis is that $\mu_{1+3} = \mu_{2+4}$, where μ_{1+3} indicates the average means of the first and third treatment populations com-bined and μ_{2+4} has comparable meaning for the second and fourth treatment populations. If the populations have equal Ns, then the algebraic version of the hypothesis would be

$$H_a: \frac{\mu_1 + \mu_3}{2} = \frac{\mu_2 + \mu_4}{2}.$$

A more general version that accommodates differences in population sizes is

$$H_a: \frac{N_1\mu_1 + N_3\mu_3}{N_1 + N_3} = \frac{N_2\mu_2 + N_4\mu_4}{N_2 + N_4}.$$

The second null hypothesis states that the mean for treatment 1 equals the mean for treatment 3 (no difference between the confident treatments). Stated formally, the hypothesis is

$$H_b: \mu_1 = \mu_3.$$

The third null hypothesis is just like the second except that it deals with the second and fourth treatments. Formally, that hypothesis is

$$H_c: \mu_2 = \mu_4 .$$

Note that we predicted no difference for our third substantive hypothesis, and so H_c is what our theory expected, whereas H_a and H_b are opposite to what our theory expected. There is some difference in the way people use the word *null* in the statistical literature. The usage throughout this book is that null means *no difference*. Some texts use the term as synonymous with *the opposite of a substantive hypothesis*. However, sometimes theory predicts explicitly that there will be no difference. In that case, the substantive hypothesis is formally a null hypothesis (no difference), and we can test such a hypothesis directly.

Orthogonal F Tests

Orthogonal contrasts involve the difference between just two means. They may represent combinations of treatment groups such as $\mu_1 + \mu_3$ versus $\mu_2 + \mu_4$. They may involve only two groups such as μ_1 versus μ_3. Or, as Exhibit 4.1 indicates, they may involve any combination of groups. Whatever the combinations represented, the contrast tests whether one mean (or combination mean) equals the other one. As you know, a t test is appropriate for the difference between a pair of means. Therefore, it is possible to conduct one t test for each of the specified contrasts.

Actually, when the numerator $df = 1$, $F = t^2$. You can check that fact easily by comparing t and F tables. For example, if $\alpha = .05$, then you would select the two-tailed test column for the t table and also select the .05 F table. Now suppose the denominator $df = 40$. The value in the t table is 2.021, whereas the value in the first column of the F table (i.e., when numerator $df = 1$) is 4.08, and $2.021^2 = 4.08$. With only two groups involved (a difference between two means), the numerator df will equal 1, and so we should be able to get comparable results doing a conventional difference-between-means t test versus doing an ANOVA type of F test.

To be consistent with the ANOVA focus of this book, we will first use the ANOVA approach: a ratio of an estimate of variance based on SS_B to one based on SS_W. Remember that the MS_W from ANOVA is a pooled estimate of the common population variance. We can use that information directly from the F table in Exhibit 3.3. Now,

Exhibit 4.2

F Test for First Contrast

SOURCE	SS	df	MS	F
Between	4.3802	1	4.3802	12.8754**
Within	14.9682	44	0.3402	

** significant at $\alpha = .01$.

however, SS_B and df_B will depend on the particular contrast being tested.

For the first contrast, we specified that groups 1 and 3 combined would be compared to groups 2 and 4 combined. As before, to calculate SS_B, you need the sum for each part of the contrast as well as the ns for each part. In this particular contrast, the sums are as follows:

$$\Sigma Y_1 + \Sigma Y_3 = 4.64 + 5.15 = 9.79$$

$$\Sigma Y_2 + \Sigma Y_4 = -.58 + -4.13 = -4.71.$$

The ns are 24 for each combined group. The sums and ns are needed for the first part of the computational formula for SS_B. The last part is the square of the grand total divided by the total n. Because all cases are used in this contrast, the grand total is 5.08 and the total n is 48. Calculations for SS_B, then, are

$$SS_B = \frac{(9.79)^2}{24} + \frac{(-4.71)^2}{24} - \frac{(5.08)^2}{48}$$

$$= 3.9935 + .9243 - .5376$$

$$= 4.3802.$$

From Exhibit 3.3, we have $SS_W = 14.9682$ with $df_W = 44$, giving $MS_W = .3402$. The F table for this contrast is shown in Exhibit 4.2. Clearly, there is a significant difference between the confident treatments (groups 1 and 3) and the hesitant treatments (groups 2 and 4). The first contrast hypothesis in its null form is rejected.

Calculations for the other two contrasts follow the same form. The second contrast involves only groups 1 and 3, and so we have sums of 4.64 and 5.15 with ns of 12 each. The total is just the sum of those sums, or 9.79 with a total n of 24.

Exhibit 4.3

F Test for Second Contrast

SOURCE	SS	df	MS	F
Between	.0108	1	.0108	.0317
Within	14.9682	44	0.3402	

$$SS_B = \frac{(4.64)^2}{12} + \frac{(5.15)^2}{12} - \frac{(9.79)^2}{24}$$

$$= 1.7941 + 2.2102 - 3.9935$$

$$= .0108.$$

Again using SS_W and df_W from Exhibit 3.3, the F table for this contrast is shown in Exhibit 4.3. There is no basis for rejecting the null hypothesis that, among the confident treatments, neat and sloppy variations do not differ in stooge evaluations.

Finally, the third contrast involves groups 2 and 4, and so we have sums of –.58 and –4.13, also with ns of 12 each. The total is –4.71 with an n of 24. Calculations are

$$SS_B = \frac{(-.58)^2}{12} + \frac{(-4.13)^2}{12} - \frac{(-4.71)^2}{24}$$

$$= .0280 + 1.4214 - .9243$$

$$= .5251.$$

The F table for this contrast is shown in Exhibit 4.4. Although this F is somewhat larger than the one we found for the second contrast, it still is well below the .05 critical level of 4.08. Consequently, we do not reject the null hypothesis that among hesitant stooges, the neat versus sloppy variations do not differ in stooge evaluations. Keep in mind that the conclusion always is in terms of the populations, not the observed samples. That is, our results lead us to believe (with 95% confidence) that if we ran everybody in existence through the experiment, we would expect that the mean confident rating would exceed the mean hesitant rating, but that the neat versus sloppy variations would not show any differences on the average.

Exhibit 4.4

F Test for Third Contrast

SOURCE	SS	df	MS	F
Between	.5251	1	.5251	1.5435
Within	14.9682	44	0.3402	

Partitioning Total Variance

Recall that the idea of ANOVA was to partition the total sum of squares and the total degrees of freedom into two separate parts: within groups and between groups. The sum of the parts equaled the total: $SS_B + SS_W = SS_T$. The contrasts we have just examined further partitioned the SS_B into three separate segments: confident versus hesitant stooges, neat versus sloppy among confident stooges, and neat versus sloppy among hesitant stooges. Because these are orthogonal contrasts and only three orthogonal contrasts are possible with just four treatments, it should be the case that the separate SS_B terms add up to the original SS_B. From the three sets of calculations, we have $4.3802 + .0108 + .5251 = 4.9161$. This agrees within rounding error with the SS_B from Exhibit 3.3.

Similarly, the degrees of freedom for the between-groups estimate of variance was $df_B = 3$ in Exhibit 3.3. The contrasts each had 1 df, and there were three contrasts. Consequently, the degrees of freedom add up to the correct total as well.

Any set of $J - 1$ orthogonal contrasts for J groups will partition both the sum of squares and the degrees of freedom into separate possible explanations of the overall variation observed in the data. As stated earlier, if possible, the contrasts should be theory driven rather than any set that comes to mind. The reason for that assertion should be more evident now. How you define the contrasts partitions the overall variance into those particular explanations. If the explanations are theoretically relevant, then the individual contrast tests speak to the reasons for making those contrast tests. If the contrasts are ad hoc, then their relevance for the underlying theory may be unclear.

Suppose instead of theoretically relevant contrasts we had used the convenient but atheoretical contrasts suggested earlier:

Contrast 1: $\mu_1 = (\mu_2 + \mu_3 + \mu_4)/3$

Contrast 2: $\mu_2 = (\mu_3 + \mu_4)/2$

Contrast 3: $\mu_3 = \mu_4$

Try doing the calculations for testing these hypotheses. You should find the following:

First contrast:	$SS_B = 1.2619$, $F = 3.7093$
Second contrast:	$SS_B = 0.0660$, $F = 0.194$
Third contrast:	$SS_B = 3.5882$, $F = 10.6085$
Total:	$SS_B = 4.9161$, as it should

As before, the critical value of F for 1 and 40 df (44, but we are using the next lower value in the table) is 4.08. Consequently, at $\alpha = .05$, we would have concluded the following:

1. Neat-confident stooges are *not* evaluated differently from any other type, although the results approach significance.
2. Neat-hesitant stooges are *not* evaluated differently from sloppy stooges.
3. Sloppy-confident stooges *are* evaluated differently from sloppy-hesitant stooges.

Now, this may be somewhat useful, but it clearly does not give the same sense of clear, strong results that the other contrasts did. We have partitioned the variance in a less useful manner. Our theoretical work will advance more rapidly if it provides the basis for the contrasts that we test.

Rules Governing Orthogonal Contrasts

How can you tell whether the contrasts that you would like to test are orthogonal? Fortunately, there are explicit rules that let you know whether a set of contrasts satisfies orthogonality. They require setting up codes for each of the variables and for each of the contrasts and then doing some very simple calculations with those codes. Exhibit 4.5 shows the codes for the first set of contrasts examined earlier.

Where did these codes come from? Their origin is very simple. The first contrast we had defined earlier was the combined confident treatments versus the combined hesitant treatments. That im-

Exhibit 4.5

Codes for Original Orthogonal Contrasts

Treatment Group		Orthogonal Codes		
		Contrast 1	Contrast 2	Contrast 3
1	Neat-Con	1	1	0
2	Neat-Hes	−1	0	1
3	Slop-Con	1	−1	0
4	Slop-Hes	−1	0	−1

plies averaging (i.e., adding up) the confident treatment scores and subtracting the average of the hesitant treatment scores. We do not need to calculate the actual means involved. The codes simply mirror what the desired contrasts would calculate. So, the first set of codes indicates to add groups 1 and 3 and subtract groups 2 and 4, and this is comparable to asking about the mean of the confident treatments combined minus the mean of the hesitant treatments combined. The second set of codes indicates to subtract the sloppy-confident treatment from the neat-confident treatment and ignore the other two groups, therefore concentrating on the difference between the two confident treatments. The third contrast does the same for the two hesitant treatments, ignoring the confident ones.

There is one set of codes for each desired contrast, and each group has its own code for each contrast. Further, the sum of the codes (i.e., the column total) for any contrast equals zero. This is a first requirement: The sum of the codes must equal zero. There is a second requirement that takes a little calculation to verify. For each *pair* of contrasts, the sum of the group-by-group product of the codes must also equal zero. Let's look at the first two contrasts. For each group, multiply the code for contrast 1 by the code for contrast 2, and then add these products over all groups. You should get

$$1 \times 1 + (-1) \times 0 + 1 \times (-1) + (-1) \times 0 = 1 + 0 - 1 + 0 = 0.$$

The product sums for the other two pairs of contrasts are

$$1 \times 0 + (-1) \times 1 + 1 \times 0 + (-1) \times (-1) = 0 \text{ for contrasts 1 and 3; and}$$

$$1 \times 0 + 0 \times 1 + (-1) \times 0 + 0 \times (-1) = 0 \text{ for contrasts 2 and 3.}$$

Exhibit 4.6

Illustration of Codes for Atheoretical Contrasts

Treatment Group	Orthogonal Codes			Products		
	C_1	C_2	C_3	C_1C_2	C_1C_3	C_2C_3
1	1	0	0	0	0	0
2	–1/3	1	0	–1/3	0	0
3	–1/3	–1/2	1	1/6	–1/3	–1/2
4	–1/3	–1/2	–1	1/6	1/3	1/2
Sums	0	0	0	0	0	0

NOTE: C = contrast.

All the product sums equal zero, and this says that all pairs of contrasts are orthogonal.

It might help, when setting up contrast codes, to include space in your table for the products. The second atheoretical set of contrasts just illustrated would generate the table shown in Exhibit 4.6. Be sure you understand why each of the codes has the value shown. Do not be confused by the fractional codes. If you were comparing the mean of Group 1 to the mean of the other three groups, then you would let Group 1 stand as is but would need to add up groups 2 through 4 and divide by 3 to get their mean. That is all the fractional codes are accomplishing. If you do not like fractions, then you could just as well let the codes for the three contrasts be as follows:

$$
\begin{array}{rrr}
3 & 0 & 0 \\
-1 & 2 & 0 \\
-1 & -1 & 1 \\
-1 & -1 & -1.
\end{array}
$$

Try checking these for orthogonality.

Technically, to ensure orthogonality, one should multiply each of the codes by the size of the group that code represents before calculating the products and sums shown in Exhibits 4.5 and 4.6. For "balanced" experimental designs (i.e., with equal ns for all groups), that simply would be unnecessary work. With the stooge data, we would have multiplied everything by 12, but the sums and the sums of products still would be zero.

For unbalanced designs (unequal ns), the process is a bit more complicated. One way in which to create codes for the first theory-driven contrast would be to use $1/(n_1 + n_3)$ for the cases in treatments 1 and 3 (confident) and $-1/(n_2 + n_4)$ for the cases in the other two treatments (hesitant). The denominators will be the sum of the ns for all groups combined for a given contrast. Suppose there had been only 10 cases in treatment 1 but 12 in each of the others. The simple 1 versus −1 coding, when multiplied by the unequal group ns, would give

$$10 \times 1 + 12 \times (-1) + 12 \times 1 + 12 \times (-1) = -2,$$

which does not satisfy the criterion that the sum of codes for a given contrast equal zero. Similarly, you would find that the sum of product criterion also would be violated. Using the reciprocal of the sum of ns for each part of a contrast will satisfy both criteria.

An alternative coding for unequal ns would be to use $(n_2 + n_4)$ for treatments 1 and 3 versus $-(n_1 + n_3)$ for treatments 2 and 4. For people who do not like fractional numbers, this may seem simplest. You have to be careful that each group's code involves only the ns from the groups with which it is contrasted. A quick check should convince you that these two approaches are simple multiples of each other and thus do exactly the same job.

When there are more than three treatments, it is easy to get confused and create contrasts that are not orthogonal. One routine that always will work is to contrast the first group with the rest, then contrast the second group with the third through the last, and so on. That procedure generates the atheoretical contrasts used in Exhibit 4.4 previously. However, you should realize that because there is nothing theoretical about such a pat set of contrasts, they hardly constitute a priori hypotheses and are not recommended without a greater understanding of the appropriate methods for testing them.

Orthogonal Contrasts via SPSS

Although the amount of work involved in computing orthogonal contrast F tests is not bad once you are used to the process, it is much easier to let SPSS do the work. The SPSS routine you need is ONEWAY, and you will need to use the CONTRAST command. Exhibit 4.7 assumes that a system file has been created with all data and labels. The three contrasts are easily specified and can be readily recognized in the program.

Exhibit 4.7

Specifying Contrasts in SPSS

```
GET FILE= 'STOOGE.SYS'.
ONEWAY VARIABLE= RATING BY GROUP (1,4)
    /CONTRAST= 1 -1  1 -1
    /CONTRAST= 1  0  1  0
    /CONTRAST= 0  1  0  1.
```

Exhibit 4.8

SPSS Contrast Results

	Value	S. Error	T Value	D.F.	T Prob
Contrast 1	1.2083	.3367	3.588	44	.001
Contrast 2	-.0425	.2381	-.178	44	.859
Contrast 3	.2958	.2381	1.242	44	.221

The results for the SPSS contrasts are shown in Exhibit 4.8. SPSS uses t tests rather than F tests for the contrasts. With 1 df in the numerator, F is equal to t^2. To check the equivalence of the two sets of results, just square the t values in Exhibit 4.8 and you will see that they equal the Fs in Exhibits 4.2, 4.3, and 4.4. Aside from avoiding hand calculations, there is one advantage of using SPSS. The probabilities shown do not depend on an F table that provides only two α levels and selected df values. The SPSS results give exact probabilities.

You could calculate t tests by hand rather than by using the F test approach or the SPSS CONTRAST command. The results should be exactly the same as those already obtained. For the first contrast, you should get the calculations shown in Exhibit 4.8. The other t tests would proceed in exactly the same way. Because MS_W is a pooled estimate of the presumed common population variance, σ, and was already calculated by ANOVA, it is easiest to use that for S_{pooled} in the formula for t.

$$t = \frac{\overline{Y}_{1+3} - \overline{Y}_{2+4}}{S_{\overline{y}_{1+3} - \overline{y}_{2+4}}}$$

where

$$\overline{Y}_{1+3} - \overline{Y}_{2+4} = .6042 \quad \text{and}$$

$$s_{(\bar{y}_{1+3}-\bar{y}_{2+4})} = s_{pooled}\sqrt{\frac{1}{12}+\frac{1}{12}} = \sqrt{MS_w}\,(.2887) = .1684;$$

$$t = \frac{.6042}{.1684} = 3.588.$$

Note that both the calculated difference between the means and the estimated standard error of that difference are exactly half the values shown in the SPSS printout. SPSS calculates slightly differently but, as is obvious, the resulting t value is correct. As noted earlier, if you square the calculated t of 3.588, you will find (within rounding error) the earlier F value of 12.8754.

Explained Variance and Effect Sizes

In our examination of the stooge data, we concluded that the treatment groups did differ, and we subsequently explored differences across subsets of groups. At our chosen level of confidence (95%, or $1 - \alpha$), we could conclude that the results are not just a consequence of random sampling fluctuation from populations with equal means. Now comes what can be thought of as either a substantive theoretical question or a practical question as opposed to a statistical one: Was there enough difference between treatments to matter?

How do we decide whether the observed difference of .65 between the combined mean for the confident groups and the combined mean for the hesitant groups is worth talking about? How about the overall spread of the means? The group means vary from .43 to −.34, giving a range of .77. Asking whether an effect is big enough to matter, or to be worth talking about, is quite different from establishing whether it could have occurred by chance.

Consider something a little more personal: your income. If your earnings increased by, say, one half of 1%, would that really matter? For someone earning $48,000 a year, that would mean a $240 increase, or $20 a month. It might buy hamburgers and fries for two, but that would hardly make much difference in one's standard of living. What would be enough to consider important—5% or 25%?

Let's turn the question around. Suppose we were talking about an increase of $1,000 a year. Would that be an important difference?

If you now earned only $5,000 a year, then you probably would say that the extra $1,000 would be great. If you were a corporate executive earning around $1 million a year, then that extra $1,000 would be only $1/10$ of 1%, a pretty trivial amount. The point is that what is important is always relative to some comparative base.

Explained Variance

We can talk about the importance of an effect in several ways, one of which is explanatory power. The term *explained variance* refers to the proportion of total variance that is attributable to some theoretical "cause." For the stooge data, the between sum of squares from ONEWAY equals 4.9162. Similarly, the within sum of squares from ONEWAY equals 14.9682. The total sum of squares is, of course, 19.8844. We could ask what proportion of the total sum of squares is accounted for by the fact that evaluations of the stooge differed systematically across treatments. The answer is a simple ratio. For the population, the ratio is called eta-squared; for the sample data, it is called E^2. For ANOVA-type data, E^2 is the proportion of the total sum of squares that is due to variation among the group means.

$$E^2 = \frac{SS_B}{SS_T} = \frac{4.9162}{19.8844} = .25.$$

E^2 is a common index of explanatory power. Its square root is called the correlation ratio. If you are familiar with similar concepts from correlation analysis, you know that r^2 is also a ratio of the "explained" sum of squares to the total sum of squares, as is R^2 for multiple regression. What does *explained* mean in this context? One way to think about it is that if all treatments had the same effect on evaluation of the stooge, then the total variance of evaluations would be quite a bit less because it would be due solely to random error. In fact, the within-group mean square (or variance estimate) from ANOVA would equal the total mean square (also a variance estimate) if there were no treatment effects. But $MS_W = .3402$, whereas $MS_T = .4231$, and the latter is considerably larger.

Clearly, the variance of the data is greater than would be expected due to factors such as individual preferences and random measurement error. To that extent, then, we can say that the treatments *explain* some proportion of the total sum of squares and that E^2 tells us what that proportion is. Because E is comparable to the correlation coefficient, r (except for not imposing a linearity assumption), the value of E often is given as an indication of the strength of effect present in the data. In this case, we have $E = .50$, which normally would be considered a fairly strong relationship. Keep in mind, however, that it is E^2 that tells us what proportion of total variance is attributable to treatment differences. If 25% is explained, then there is still 75% of the variance that must be attributable to other factors such as individual subject tastes and random measurement error.

The Effect Size Coefficient

An alternative way of documenting the effect of an independent variable is to calculate what is called an *effect size coefficient*. The common symbol for effect size is f, and we will use that notation here. Do not confuse it with the F distribution used for significance tests. Although closely related to the notion of explained variance, effect size coefficients standardize the variation due to an independent variable by dividing by the standard deviation of error. The result is a coefficient that expresses effects in a standardized form that can be readily compared across studies.

For an ANOVA, the population effect size can be thought of as the ratio of the standard deviation of the means (the square root of MS_B) to the within-groups standard deviation (the square root of MS_W). This approach, which is in keeping with the definition offered by Cohen (1988), automatically norms the variation due to treatment effect by the overall amount of random (unexplained) variation. Not all authors use that definition, however. For example, Hurlburt (1994) uses effect size to refer simply to an unstandardized difference between a pair of treatments.

We already know that an estimate of the variance of the means can be obtained from SS_B and that an estimate of the error variance in the population can be obtained from SS_W. Similar to what was done for calculating E^2, we can use the ratio of these two sums of squares rather than doing the calculating needed for separate estimates of the standard deviation of the means and the standard deviation of error. Because the effect size, f, is expressed in standard deviation form, however, we will need the square root of that ratio:

$$f = \sqrt{\frac{SS_B}{SS_W}} = \sqrt{\frac{4.9162}{14.9682}} = .57.$$

There is one minor difference between these calculations and those implied by Cohen's (1988) definition of a ratio of σ_B to σ_W. Suppose we treat the data set as a population rather than as a sample, where the population means will replace sample means and the population sizes will replace sample sizes. Let the sums of squares, SS_B and SS_W, represent the population sums. Then f as the ratio of two population variances turns out to be just a ratio of those two sums of squares. The following equations demonstrate that fact:

$$\sigma_B^2 = \frac{\sum_j (\mu_j - \mu)^2}{J} \; ; \; j = 1 .. J$$

$$= \frac{SS_B}{JN_j} \text{ if } N_j \text{ is constant for all } j$$

$$= \frac{SS_B}{N} .$$

Similarly,

$$\sigma_W^2 = \frac{SS}{N} ,$$

and so

$$\frac{\sigma_B^2}{\sigma_W^2} = \frac{SS_B}{SS_W} .$$

On the other hand, if we treat the data as sample evidence (which, of course, they are) and make *estimates* of σ_B^2 and σ_W^2, then the denominator for SS_B will be $n - k$ whereas the denominator for SS_W will be $n - 1$, and the ratio of estimates will be slightly different from SS_B / SS_W. For our four treatments with 12 cases per treatment, the denominators would be 44 and 47, respectively, and the sample estimate approach would result in an effect size of .59 instead of the .57 we got using just the sums of squares. The sum-of-squares approach provides a statement of the effect size *in the observed data*, whereas the ratio of estimates of variance provides a statement of the *estimated effect size in the population*.

How do we interpret the effect size coefficient? It literally says that the standard deviation of the group means is a bit over one half of the standard deviation of cases within the groups. Remember that the latter estimates the population standard deviation without the systematic effects of the treatents; it is the standard deviation of errors. Thus our results show that the effect of the treatments is about half the standard deviation of errors.

Rules of thumb recommended by Cohen (1988) suggest that an effect size coefficient between .10 and .25 be considered small, one between .25 and .50 be considered medium, and one above .50 be considered large. Recognize that these are arbitrary standards and should be interpreted in terms of the theoretical relevance of whatever effect size for the work you are doing. By Cohen's criteria, stooge role had a large effect on the evaluations made by the naive subjects.

There is some difference across disciplines in whether effect sizes or explained variances are preferred in research reports. Because they are closely related, either can be used as long as it is interpreted correctly. In fact, as Cohen (1988, p. 281) has commented, a little algebra will show that

$$f = \sqrt{\frac{E^2}{1 - E^2}}$$

or that

$$E = \sqrt{\frac{f^2}{1 + f^2}} \ .$$

Although E and f are approximately equal in the stooge study, that will be true primarily when f is small. As the strength of effect increases, f increases faster than does E. For an f of .9, for example, E would equal only .67. There is a third important concept closely related to explained variance and effect size: that of statistical power. A discussion of power appears inChapter 7.

Summary

The major concern of this chapter has been how to decide just where significant effects occur in observed data. A one-way ANOVA simply says whether, overall, the observed group means differ enough to conclude that the population means are not the same. Finding a significant F, however, does not imply that all population means are different from each other. It simply says that the total variance in the observed data, compared to the within-group variance, is larger than would be expected by chance if all populations had the same mean.

One can explore whether there are significant differences among particular subsets of treatments by using contrasts. Ideally, contrasts are defined on the basis of substantive theory prior to examination of empirical results. Then there is no chance that something is tested simply because it looks promising after the fact. Also, ideally, contrasts will be orthogonal, or uncorrelated with each other. There are easy rules to follow in determining whether a set of contrasts is orthogonal. Although theory-based contrasts and orthogonal contrasts both are preferable, it is possible to conduct a posteriori tests and nonorthogonal tests, but these require much more stringent F levels to guard against erosion of the chosen α level.

Two related questions were addressed in addition to creating and testing contrasts. First, how much effect do we need before we can consider it to be important in substantive or practical terms? That question is answered either in explained variance terms via E^2 or in effect size terms via the coefficient f. The two are precisely related by simple formulas.

5 Analyzing More Than One Factor

Let's reconsider the data from the stooge experiment. As you may recall, there really were two substantive research hypotheses that guided the design of the experiments:

Hypothesis 1: An actor's apparent confidence during a problem-focused discussion will influence others' opinions of the quality of the actor's contributions to that discussion.

Hypothesis 2: An actor's appearance (how well he or she dresses) during a problem-focused discussion will influence others' opinions of the quality of the actor's contributions to that discussion.

With two separate dimensions, however, there is implicitly a third hypothesis:

Hypothesis 3: Appearance and apparent confidence do not interact in their effects on others' opinions of the quality of the actor's contributions.

For the purposes of ANOVA, of course, the statistical hypotheses to be tested must be in the null form. Specifically:

Hypothesis 1: $\mu_{confident} = \mu_{hesitant}$.

Hypothesis 2: $\mu_{neat} = \mu_{sloppy}$.

Hypothesis 3: Appearance and confidence do not interact.

Recall from Chapter 1 that if two or more factors are perfectly independent in their effects on the dependent variable, then they do not interact. For two factors, then, the effects of each level of one factor can be added to the effects of each level of the other factor to predict the dependent variable for that particular combination of factor levels. Interaction, on the other hand, means that particular combinations of factor levels produce unique, nonadditive consequences for the dependent variable. The result, which may not be immediately obvious, would be that the means in the various cells of a table cross-classifying the different treatment levels would vary more than would be expected on the basis of additive effects.

Expanding ANOVA

When we analyzed the data in Chapter 3 using one-way ANOVA, the results confirmed the less explicit hypothesis that the four treatments influenced others' opinions differentially. Because the experiment really manipulated two dimensions rather than one, one-way ANOVA did not provide a complete picture. The orthogonal comparisons indicated that the confident-hesitant variation had a significant effect on evaluations of the stooge, whereas the neat-sloppy variation did not. In an indirect way, those comparisons constituted separate tests of the null versions of Hypotheses 1 and 2. Not only was such a procedure inefficient, however, but it also ignored the third hypothesis: whether confidence and appearance interact.

Expanding the Formal Model

Any experimental design that cross-classifies all values of two or more factors is called a *factorial* design. Exhibit 5.1 shows the factorial design for the stooge experiment, making explicit the two-factor character of the study rather than the simple one-way design analyzed earlier. The cell entries show the relevant population means being estimated by the experimental data. Consider the null hypotheses just stated. Hypothesis 1 pertains to the marginal means of the columns in the table (confidence without reference to appearance), Hypothesis 2 pertains to the means of the rows (appearance without reference to confidence), and Hypothesis 3 pertains to the pattern of the individual cell means inside the table. It should be evident to you that adding new factors to such a design can rapidly expand the number of subjects and sessions needed for a complete set of experiments. For example, if we wanted to add the factor of stooge gender, then there would be a three-dimensional table with each dimension having two variations: confident versus hesitant stooge, neat versus sloppy stooge, and female versus male stooge.

Exhibit 5.1

A Two-Factor Factorial Model

		Confidence		Total
		Confident	Hesitant	
Appearance	Neat	$\mu_{neat\text{-}con}$	$\mu_{neat\text{-}hes}$	μ_{neat}
	Sloppy	$\mu_{slop\text{-}con}$	$\mu_{slop\text{-}hes}$	μ_{slop}
Total		μ_{con}	μ_{hes}	μ_{total}

Keeping 12 cases for each of the 8 cells and continuing to have 3 naive subjects per session, we would need 32 sessions and a total of 96 naive subjects.

If our theoretical considerations led us to add a fourth dichotomous dimension, then we would need 64 sessions and 192 subjects. If each dimension had more than two variations, then the expansion of cells in the table would be even more rapid. For now, keep in mind that although expanding the logic of ANOVA to two, three, or more factors is straightforward, actually conducting multiple-factor studies using complete factorial designs can become very costly.

Let's reexamine the stooge data, this time in a table with two rows for the two variations of stooge neatness and two columns for the two variations of stooge confidence. Exhibit 5.2 shows plots of the data arranged in that manner. As before, the dotted lines represent the overall mean of the data, whereas the solid lines represent the mean of the data for each cell.

More About the Idea of Statistical Interaction

Interaction is most easily explained in terms of its absence. As noted before, if confidence and appearance do not interact, then the effects of confidence and the effects of appearance are separate and additive; neither affects how the other operates on the dependent variable. Exhibit 5.3 shows what the cell means actually were from the stooge experiment versus what they would have to be if the overall mean

Exhibit 5.2

Two-Way Plot of the Stooge Data

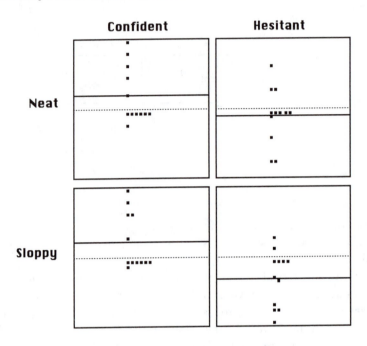

and the row and column effects stayed the same but there were no interaction. Each entry is calculated by starting with the overall mean, adding the difference between the overall mean and that row's mean, and also adding the difference between the overall mean and that column's mean. In equation form,

$$\overline{X}_{rc} = \overline{X}_T + (\overline{X}_r - \overline{X}_T) + (\overline{X}_c - \overline{X}_T). \qquad (5.1)$$

The subscripts indicate total (T), which row (r), and which column (c). For the neat/confident cell of the table, the calculations (using accuracy of just two decimal places) are based on an overall mean of .11 plus a row effect of (.17 − .11) plus a column effect of (.41 − .11). Thus the predicted cell mean under the hypothesis of independence is .11 + .06 + .30 = .47. Entries for the other cells under independence are obtained in the same manner.

Note that the observed cell means are not too different from those expected under the independence hypothesis. Each cell mean departs an absolute .07 to .09 from its expected value. The neat-confident

Exhibit 5.3

Observed Versus Independent Cell Means

	Confident	Hesitant	
Neat	Observed: .39 Independent: .11 + (.17 − .11) + (.41 − .11) = .47	Observed: −.05 Independent: .11 + (.17 − .11) + (−.20 − .11) = −.14	.17
Sloppy	Observed: .43 Independent: .11 + (.04 − .11) + (.41 − .11) = .34	Observed: −.34 Independent: .11 + (.04 − .11) + (−.20 − .11) = −.27	.04
	.41	−.20	.11

and sloppy-hesitant cells have lower means than expected, whereas the neat-hesitant and sloppy-confident means are higher than expected. The statistical question, of course, is whether these departures from expectation under the independence hypothesis are sufficient to reject that hypothesis.

Hypothesis 3 can be reexpressed in terms of row and column effect parameters:

$$\mu_{rc} = \mu + \beta_r + \beta_c \tag{5.2}$$

where

μ_{rc} is the population mean for some particular combination of appearance (the row factor, subscripted r) and confidence (the column factor, subscripted c),

μ is, again, the overall population mean,

β_r is the effect of appearance level r,

β_c is the effect of confidence level c, and

$\Sigma\beta_r = \Sigma\beta_c = 0$.

As with Equation 5.1, Equation 5.2 says that we simply add the effects of the separate treatments to the overall mean. Therefore, we are assuming that stooge confidence will not work differently for different appearances and, similarly, that appearances will not have different effects for the different levels of stooge confidence. As with the one-way model, the separate row effects, $\Sigma\beta_r$, must add to zero, as must the separate column effects $\Sigma\beta_c$.

For a general model that allows for both factors and interaction, we need one more β term to account for the interaction:

$$\mu_{rc} = \mu + \beta_r + \beta_c + \beta_{rc}$$

$$\Sigma\beta_{rc} = 0. \tag{5.3}$$

Note that Equation 5.3 is simply Equation 5.2 with an added term. The β_{rc} term allows the model to predict cell means that not only have some overall effect of appearance, β_r, and some overall effect of confidence, β_c, but also have a unique effect of any particular combination of those two factors working together. As with the row and column effects, the β_{rc} terms representing unique cell effects must sum to zero.

The Two-Way ANOVA Model

Basic Equations

Following Equation 5.3, we can specify the prediction for each observation (i.e., each case) as

$$Y_{irc} = \mu + \beta_r + \beta_c + \beta_{rc} + e_{irc}, \tag{5.4}$$

which says that any observation contains an overall mean effect, plus the additive effects of the row factor, plus the additive effects of the column factor, plus joint effects of the particular combination of row and column factors (interaction), plus random error.

If you think through Equation 5.4 carefully in terms of the 2×2 design of the stooge experiments, you will realize that there are two different values of the β_r, one for each row of Exhibit 5.1. Similarly, there are two different values of the β_c, one for each column of the table. Finally, there are four different values of β_{rc}, one for each cell of the table. Altogether, then, there are eight β values implied by Equation 5.4. With a 2×2 table, the two values of β_r are equal except for their signs, as are the two values of β_c and the four values of β_{rc}. However, with more rows and columns, the separate values of the β_r, the β_c, and the β_{rc} all can have unique departures from their expected values under the hypothesis of independence.

In general, if there are R rows and C columns in the table, then there will be $R + C + RC$ different values of β implied by the three effect hypotheses. For a 2×3 experimental design, there would be $2 + 3 + 6 = 11$ different β values, and so on. If there is no interaction

(Hypothesis 3), then all the values of β_{rc} for the RC different treatment cells will equal zero, and their estimates from the sample data will be zero except for minor variations due to random sampling. If there is no overall row effect, then the R values of β_r also will be zero. If there is no overall column effect, then the C values of β_c will be zero. Do we really have to make estimates of all β values and test each of them before deciding whether the hypotheses are plausible?

Fortunately, a two 2-way analysis of variance allows testing all row effects together in 1 test, testing all column effects together in 1 test, and testing all cell (interaction) effects together in 1 test. That is, there is 1 test for each of the three hypotheses. It is far more convenient to have just the 3 tests rather than 8 or 11 or however many different ones.

In the one-way ANOVA model, we found that the overall sum of squares for Y, the dependent variable, can be divided into variation between groups (or treatments, for experimental usage) and variation within groups. That is, variation can be partitioned into that portion which can be explained by experimental manipulation versus that portion which cannot be so explained. For the one-way case, there were only two explanations for observed variation: group differences versus random variation. Therefore, there could be only two partitions: $SS_{between}$ and SS_{within} groups. Similarly, the total degrees of freedom were partitioned into $df_{between}$ and df_{within}. We then were able to construct two estimates of variance that should agree with each other if the factor had no effect, that is, if all the β_j of the one-way model were equal to zero.

The between-means estimate was based on variation among the group means, weighted by sample size, to be a true estimate of the population variance. The within-groups estimate involved pooling within-group variation across all groups. An F test determined whether, within a specified level of confidence, these two estimates agreed. If they did, then there was no reason to reject the hypothesis that the population means were equal; hence we could conclude that the treatment had no effect. If the estimates did not agree, then there was reason to reject the null hypothesis of no effect in favor of the alternative that the population means really did differ. Note in particular that the within-groups estimate of variance is automatically free of the effects of any treatment because it is calculated entirely within the treatment groups.

Because we now have three hypotheses rather than one, we will need to partition SS_{total} into four parts: (a) that part due to row effects (stooge confidence), (b) that part due to column effects (stooge appearance), (c) that part due to row-column interaction effects, and (d) that part attributable to random variation. For each partition, there will be an appropriate sum of squares and an appropriate degrees of freedom. Therefore, *each partition can contribute an independent estimate of variance.*

Under the hypothesis that the row factor has no effect, differences among the row means should be due entirely to random sampling variation around the overall mean. Similarly, if the column factor has no effect, then differences among the column means should be due to random sampling variation. Finally, if there is no interaction, then differences between the cell means and what would be expected by simply adding row and column effects should be due only to random sampling variation. Each of the three hypotheses for the two-way analysis can be seen in terms of comparing an estimate of variance associated with that hypothesis to an estimate of variance based on pure random variation within the cells. Exhibit 5.4 shows the equations for all of the sums of squares and degrees of freedom. Although these look pretty messy, they are direct equivalents of the equations developed in the one-way model.

The four partitions of SS_T (total sum of squares) will be SS_R (row sum of squares), SS_C (column sum of squares), SS_I (interaction sum of squares), and SS_E (error sum of squares). Calling the last partition *error* is standard terminology, but you should realize that we mean error only in the sense that the variation is unexplained by our theory, not in the sense of a mistake. Just as with the within-groups sum of squares for one-way ANOVA, the error sum of squares will be free of any effects of the three hypothesized factors because it will be calculated within each of the treatment cells and pooled over all cells. Therefore, it makes an appropriate basis of comparison for the three estimates of variance that relate to the hypotheses. Notice, by the way, that including the error sum of squares means there always will be one more partition of SS_T than we have hypotheses.

Working Through the Data

It will be convenient to do the calculations for the various sums and sums of squares first so that the necessary pieces of data are ready to plug into the formulas. Exhibit 5.5 shows the results of those calculations.

Exhibit 5.4

Sums of Squares and Degrees of Freedom for a Two-Way ANOVA

Sums of Squares	Degrees of Freedom
$SS_T = \sum_i \sum_r \sum_c Y_{irc}^2 - \dfrac{\left(\sum_i \sum_r \sum_c Y_{irc}\right)^2}{n}$	$df_T = n - 1$
$SS_R = \sum_r \dfrac{\left(\sum_i \sum_c Y_{irc}\right)^2}{n_r} - \dfrac{\left(\sum_i \sum_r \sum_c Y_{irc}\right)^2}{n}$	$df_R = R - 1$
$SS_C = \sum_c \dfrac{\left(\sum_i \sum_r Y_{irc}\right)^2}{n_c} - \dfrac{\left(\sum_i \sum_r \sum_c Y_{irc}\right)^2}{n}$	$df_C = C - 1$
$SS_E = \sum_i \sum_r \sum_c Y_{irc}^2 - \sum_r \sum_c \dfrac{\left(\sum_i Y_{irc}\right)^2}{n_{rc}}$	$df_E = n - RC$
$SS_I = SS_T - SS_R - SS_C - SS_E$	$df_I = (R-1)(C-1)$

The total sum of squares is calculated without reference to any treatments. Therefore, it ignores rows, columns, and individual cells of the table and simply treats all cases together. Consequently, it is calculated exactly as it was for the one-way model. The difference in the equation for SS_T shown in Exhibit 5.4 versus that shown in Equation 3.9 for one-way ANOVA is due to our adding one dimension to the experimental design table. Now, instead of simply adding over cases and groups (subscripts ij for the one-way model), we add over cases, rows, and columns. Because both rows and columns define different treatment groups, we no longer can simply talk about adding over groups.

The first term for SS_T says to square each value of Y and add those squared values for all cases in all rows and columns. For the stooge experiments, that sum of all squared values of Y is in the lower right-hand part of Exhibit 5.5. It equals 20.4220, as we found in Chapter 3. The second term of the equation for SS_T says to add all values of Y for all cases, square that sum, and then divide by the

Exhibit 5.5

*n*s, Sums, and Sums of Squares From the Experimental Results

	Confident	*Hesitant*	
Neat	$n = 12$ $\Sigma Y = 4.64$ $\Sigma Y^2 = 5.5896$	$n = 12$ $\Sigma Y = -.58$ $\Sigma Y^2 = 3.7564$	$n = 24$ $\Sigma Y = 4.06$ $\Sigma Y^2 = 9.3460$
Sloppy	$n = 12$ $\Sigma Y = 5.15$ $\Sigma Y^2 = 6.0725$	$n = 12$ $\Sigma Y = -4.13$ $\Sigma Y^2 = 5.0035$	$n = 24$ $\Sigma Y = 1.02$ $\Sigma Y^2 = 11.0760$
	$n = 24$ $\Sigma Y = 9.79$ $\Sigma Y^2 = 11.6621$	$n = 24$ $\Sigma Y = -4.71$ $\Sigma Y^2 = 8.7599$	$n = 48$ $\Sigma Y = 5.08$ $\Sigma Y^2 = 20.4220$

total number of cases in the sample. The square of the sum of all values of Y divided by total n is $(5.08)^2/48 = .5376$, as was found in Chapter 3. The difference is 19.8844, and this agrees with what we already knew for these data.

The total sum of squares for any given data set always will be the same, regardless of how that sum is partitioned among possible explanatory effects. As before, total df equals $n - 1$, where n is the total number of cases in all treatments combined. Incidentally, all sums of squares must be non-negative (either positive or zero). Any time you end up with a negative sum of squares, you must have made a computational error somewhere.

Parallel to the between-groups calculation for the one-way model, both the row main effect sum of squares and the column main effect sum of squares can be defined theoretically as follows:

$$SS_R = \sum_r \frac{(\bar{Y}_r - \bar{Y})^2}{n_t}$$

$$SS_C = \sum_c \frac{(\bar{Y}_c - \bar{Y})^2}{n_c}$$

As is usual for variance calculations, the computational formulas shown in Exhibit 5.4 are algebraically equivalent to the theoretical version but are much easier to use. These computations usually are done via computer software. However, it helps your understanding of what ANOVA is all about to work through what computations the formulas require. The calculations for SS_R, using the appropriate equation in Exhibit 5.4 and data from Exhibit 5.5, are as follows:

$$SS_R = \frac{4.06^2}{24} + \frac{1.02^2}{24} - \frac{5.08^2}{48}$$

$$= .6868 + .0434 - .5376$$

$$= .1926.$$

The row sums are 4.06 and 1.02, respectively. The row ns each are 24, and the second part of the equation is exactly as already calculated for SS_T. In fact, you should note that the equations for SS_R, SS_C, and SS_T all have the same second term. Finally, $df_R = R - 1 = 2 - 1 = 1$.

Next, calculate SS_C. The first term of SS_C says to square each column total and divide that value by the number of cases in that column. Then add those results over all columns. The second term, as noted earlier, is the same as that for SS_T and SS_R, and so it already has been calculated. The column sums are 9.79 and −4.71, respectively, and again the ns each are 24. Calculations are as follows:

$$SS_C = \frac{9.79^2}{24} + \frac{-4.71^2}{24} - \frac{5.08^2}{48}$$

$$= 3.9935 + .9243 - .5376$$

$$= 4.3802.$$

Degrees of freedom is $df_C = C - 1 = 2 - 1 = 1$.

We now have expressions for the total sum of squares and two of the partitions. All we need is a formula for calculating one of the remaining two, and then the other can be obtained by subtraction. The simpler of the two remaining sums of squares is SS_E, or the error sum of squares. The computational formula is shown in Exhibit 5.4. There are two important things to notice about the formula for SS_E. The first term is exactly like the first term for SS_T, which we already have calculated. The second term, however, is something new. It says that for each cell in the table, square the sum for that cell, divide by the number of cases in the cell, and add up those figures over all cells. The cell sums are 4.64, −.58, 5.15, and −4.13. All cells have 12 cases. Calculations are as follows, borrowing 20.4220 from our earlier calculation of SS_T.

Exhibit 5.6

Analysis of Variance

Source	SS	df	MS	F
Rows	.1926	1	.1926	.5661
Columns	4.3802	1	4.3802	12.8754
Interaction	.3434	1	.3434	1.0094
Error	14.9682	44	.3402	
Total	19.8844	47		

$$SS_E = 20.4220 - \left(\frac{4.64^2}{12} + \frac{-.58^2}{12} + \frac{5.15^2}{12} + \frac{-4.13^2}{12} \right)$$

$$= 20.4220 - 5.4538$$

$$= 14.9682.$$

Degrees of freedom is $df_E = n - R \times C = 48 - 2 \times 2 = 44$.

Once these four SS values have been calculated, the remaining SS_I can be found by subtraction:

$$SS_I = SS_T - SS_C - SS_R - SS_E.$$

Degrees of freedom for interaction can also be obtained by subtraction or by directly calculating $df_I = (R - 1)(C - 1) = (2 - 1)(2 - 1) = 1$.

The Two-Way ANOVA Table

We finally are ready to construct an ANOVA table and calculate the various F tests. Exhibit 5.6 shows the table with the necessary sums of squares, degrees of freedom, mean squares, and F values. This table is exactly parallel to the one-way table except that it contains separate tests for each of the three hypotheses.

Keep in mind that the mean square for error, MS_E, is the only estimate of σ^2 (the population variance) that is free from all experimental design effects (i.e., free from row, column, and interaction effects). Therefore, it provides the proper comparative basis for assessing the other sums of squares. Each of the mean squares constitutes an estimate of population variance only if the relevant null hypothesis is true. Therefore, each F ratio should be within sampling variation of unity only if the null hypothesis that gives rise to that ratio is true.

All of the tests in this particular experimental design will involve 1 and 44 *df*. For α = .05, the critical value of *F*, for 1 and 44 *df*, is 4.06. For α = .01, the critical value of *F* is 7.21. Let's look at interaction first. The *F* value for interaction shown in Exhibit 5.6 is only 1.0094. Clearly, the interaction is not significant. If it were, then interpreting the row and column main effects would be more difficult. If interaction were present, then any given row effect would be confounded by how cells in that row interact with the column effects. Similarly, any given column is confounded by how its cells interact with the row effects. Consequently, we either would say we cannot sort out the main effects or would have to decide that, say, row effects were theoretically (i.e., logically) prior to column effects, or vice versa, or that effects were simultaneous. Then we could assign the consequences of interaction accordingly. That discussion requires more than space allows, but keep in mind that when interaction is present, interpreting results becomes an issue of theoretical priority.

The two main effect *F* values shown in Exhibit 5.6 are .5661 for stooge appearance and 12.8754 for stooge confidence. We can conclude that the neatness effect is not significant, whereas the confidence effect is significant beyond the .01 level. We now have a clear picture of the effects of the two dimensions in the stooge study: The stooge's neatness does not significantly affect evaluations of his or her performance, confidence clearly does have a significant effect, and the two dimensions do not interact.

Assumptions

The assumptions of two-way ANOVA are simply extensions of those for one-way ANOVA. They are summarized in Exhibit 5.7. Obviously, it would be virtually impossible to satisfy all of these assumptions exactly in any research project. Even if a variable is approximately normally distributed in a population, it most likely is not exactly so. Even if variances are more or less equal across the populations represented by the cells of the research design, they generally will vary somewhat. Further, many of the dependent variables we wish to use might not satisfy the technical criteria for equal interval measurement.

The equal interval measurement criterion already has been discussed regarding the stooge study. Evaluations of the stooge's questions were obtained by subjects putting check marks on a line divided into five equal-sized segments and labeled *very good, some-*

Exhibit 5.7

Assumptions of Two-Way ANOVA

---

1. One *interval level* dependent variable (we have called that variable Y).

2. Two *nominal level* factors (X_1 and X_2, or row and column factors, in our usage).

3. *Independence*. The random samples from each of the subpopulations created by cross-classifying the two nominal factors are selected independently.

4. *Normality*. The dependent variable is normally distributed in all subpopulations.

5. *Homoscedasticity*. All subpopulations have the same variance.

---

what good, average, somewhat poor, and *very poor*. Responses to these items cannot be considered to be strictly equal interval because at least some subjects may not think that the subjective distance between *very* and *somewhat* is the same as the subjective distance between *somewhat* and *average*. However, both the equal-appearing interval character of the line and the normal usage of terms for most people argue that the evaluation scale is very close to satisfying the equal interval criterion.

What about the other assumptions? The stooge study used two nominal factors: appearance and confidence. Subjects were assigned randomly to treatment, and so the criterion of independent random samples was satisfied. That leaves the assumptions of normality and homoscedasticity. There are ways in which to test each of these assumptions; appropriate procedures are available in SPSS as they are in most statistical packages. Discussion of those tests is beyond the scope of this book but can be found in more advanced treatments.

To what extent can we use ANOVA if we do not satisfy its assumptions? It is comforting to know that the F test is what statisticians call *robust*. Moderate deviations from the assumptions of the test will not impair the accuracy of the F distribution. If there are minor differences across cell variances, if Y shows modest deviations from normality, or if the dependent variable is not precisely an equal interval level variable, then the F test, and thus ANOVA, will in general provide good tests of the null hypotheses. The F test is sufficiently robust that it has been used widely and appropriately for generations of research, especially experimental research. You should understand the assumptions underlying ANOVA so that you do not grossly misuse the procedure, but do not be scared off by those assumptions.

Effect Sizes

Using the data of Exhibit 5.6, it is easy to calculate effect sizes of the different tests. Following the approach for one-way ANOVA, the effect size coefficient, f, can be calculated as the ratio of the relevant sum of squares for the particular effect divided by the sum of squares for error.

$$f_{neatness} = \sqrt{\frac{.1926}{14.9682}} = .1134$$

$$f_{confidence} = \sqrt{\frac{4.3802}{14.9682}} = .5410$$

$$f_{interaction} = \sqrt{\frac{.3434}{14.9682}} = .1515.$$

As pointed out earlier, Cohen (1988) suggests that an effect size of from .10 to .25 be considered small, from .25 to .50 be considered medium, and .50 or above be considered large. By these standards, the neatness and interaction effects qualify for small effects. The effect size for confidence is .54, which by those standards is a large effect.

Extending to Three or More Factors

The way in which we extended ANOVA from one-way to two-way can readily be generalized to indicate how three or more factors can be accommodated. A third factor, for example, would mean we would have the equivalent of one two-way table for each category of the third factor, all in one three-dimensional table.

In this chapter, we have treated appearance and confidence as two separate, cross-classified dimensions. If we had hypothesized that yet another factor might affect the ratings of the stooge roles, then we could add that dimension to the experimental design and, of necessity, to the calculations and table for ANOVA. For example, suppose we hypothesized that gender of the contributor (i.e., the stooge in our experiments) could be a factor in how the naive subjects would rate presumably objective contributions. That would require a three-way data structure containing two variations of neatness by two variations of confidence by two genders: a $2 \times 2 \times 2$ table. There now would be eight cells in the experimental design,

Exhibit 5.8

Schematic of a Three-Factor Experiment

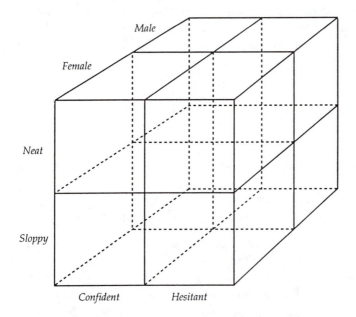

and we would have to run twice as many sessions compared to the four-cell two-way design. If we kept 12 cases per cell, then we would have to double the number of subjects as well as the laboratory time. Increasing the complexity of the design can have definite cost consequences.

As the design increases in complexity, the basic sums and sums of squares for ANOVA will be quite similar to what already has been discussed, but there will be one more main effect and potentially many more interactions to test as each new factor is added. Exhibit 5.8 shows a schematic diagram of a three-way stooge experiment. There now are three dimensions, which we will call rows (stooge appearance), columns (stooge confidence), and strata (stooge gender). If we wrote out all the equations, the subscripts would have to be $r = 1 .. R$ for rows, $c = 1 .. C$ for columns, and $s = 1 .. S$ for strata. A more common term is *files*, but that would give us another f and another F to keep track of. Notation for complex models can get to be quite a problem.

We will not actually do any formulas and computations here, but let's consider all possible hypotheses and what they would imply

Exhibit 5.9

Hypotheses for a Three-Factor Stooge Experiment

Hypothesis 1: Stooge neatness has no effect. $\mu_{neat} = \mu_{sloppy}$

Hypothesis 2: Stooge confidence has no effect. $\mu_{confident} = \mu_{hesitant}$

Hypothesis 3: Stooge gender has no effect. $\mu_{female} = \mu_{male}$

Hypothesis 4: Stooge neatness and stooge confidence do not interact. $\mu_{rc} = \mu + (\mu_r - \mu) + (\mu_c - \mu)$

Hypothesis 5: Stooge neatness and stooge gender do not interact. $\mu_{rs} = \mu + (\mu_r - \mu) + (\mu_s - \mu)$

Hypothesis 6: Stooge confidence and stooge gender do not interact. $\mu_{cs} = \mu + (\mu_c - \mu) + (\mu_s - \mu)$

Hypothesis 7: The three factors together do not interact. $\mu_{rcs} = \mu + (\mu_r - \mu) + (\mu_c - \mu) + (\mu_s - \mu)$

for computations. As before, the hypotheses will be stated in null, or no-effect, form. Exhibit 5.9 specifies the null hypotheses to be tested. Word versions of all hypotheses are specified in the left-hand portion of Exhibit 5.8; the formal equations for those hypotheses are in the right-hand portion. As noted, the subscripts r, c, and s refer to row, column, and stratum, respectively.

There are seven distinct hypotheses rather than three, even though we added only one factor. Any N-way ANOVA will contain, in addition to the obvious main effect hypotheses, all possible two-way interactions, all possible three-way interactions, and so forth up to a single N-way interaction. Clearly, as factors are added to the design, the number of interactions increases rapidly.

There always will be a total sum of squares, calculated in the same way regardless of the number of factors involved. For each factor, there will be a main effect hypothesis, hence a sum of squares calculated similarly to that for the row or column effects in the two-way model. Also, there will be separate degrees of freedom for each main effect. The interaction sums of squares and degrees of freedom get a bit more complicated, but they follow a logic similar to that for a two-way model.

From a substantive or theoretical point of view, it is easy to consider expanding the design even further. Suppose we were concerned not only with neatness, confidence, and gender of the stooge but also with the gender of the naive subjects. How women respond to a confident woman versus a hesitant woman might be different from how men might respond to her. Similarly, how women respond to a sloppy male versus a neat male might be different from how men might respond to him. Indeed, we might have good theoretical reason to expect some complex interaction effects here.

We now would have a four-way data structure: two variations of neatness, two of confidence, two of stooge gender, and two of subject gender. The main consequence in terms of the formal analysis of variance will be to expand the interaction tests greatly. With four factors, there will be 6 two-way interactions, 4 three-way interactions, and 1 four-way interaction, in addition to the 4 main effects, for a total of 15 distinct hypotheses. If you like mathematical puzzles, then you might prove to yourself that these numbers are from the binomial series.

We will end this chapter with what should be fairly obvious by now. As you increase the complexity of the research design to be analyzed by ANOVA, you generate more and more treatment cells. With only a handful of cases per cell, you still need a large number of cases to fill out the design. Further, if you are using a large survey data set such as a national sample, even though you might have plenty of cases, there can be problems of maintaining relatively similar numbers of cases in each of the cells. For experiments, we can ensure that cell sizes are identical, but that may be far from true for survey data. Unfortunately, as the number of cases per cell becomes increasingly variable, the assignment of degrees of freedom to the various main and interaction effects becomes problematic, and the accuracy of the F tests may suffer.

Is there any way to have four or five or more factors without needing so many cases? Yes, there are experimental designs that allow testing main effects, but not all interactions, in such a way that the total number of cases can be kept more manageable. These designs are discussed briefly in Chapter 6. For now, be sure you understand the two-way model we have been discussing.

Summary

The logic of the ANOVA is easily extended to as many factors as may be needed to test multiple-factor theories. The procedure provides very powerful statistical reasoning concerning whether any particular factor or combination of factors has affected a dependent variable.

With a complete factorial experimental design, it is possible to test one hypothesis for each factor, one hypothesis for each two-factor interaction, one hypothesis for each three-factor interaction, and so on depending on how many factors are included altogether.

Expanding ANOVA poses no problems at the level of either substantive theory or statistical logic. Theory is bounded only by our knowledge of the substantive area, our ability to understand increasingly complex ideas, and our ingenuity. A theory can be as complete as needed to do justice to the subject of inquiry, although there may well be reasons to keep theory relatively simple and "elegant." Similarly, there is no constraint on the logic of the ANOVA design. We can add as many factors as we want and easily work out the needed sums of squares and degrees of freedom for the various main and interaction effects. Computer programs, if they are made flexible enough, can do all the necessary calculations virtually in an instant.

Some cautions are necessary, however, when considering multiple-factor ANOVA research designs. First, as the number of factors increases, the number of cells in the factorial table representing all possible combinations of the different categories of all those factors increases very rapidly. A balanced and completely crossed research design has the same number of cases in each cell and has one cell for every combination of factors possible.

For multiple-factor experiments, only a few cases per cell can nevertheless require a very large number of subjects and an exhausting number of separate experimental sessions. For application of ANOVA to survey or other nonexperimental data, the same problem exists as to the necessary number of subjects, although there is no parallel problem of running large numbers of experimental sessions. In either case, the demands of a complex, multiple-factor design imply rapidly increasing costs of doing the necessary research.

There is a different problem for nonexperimental, multiple-factor designs. With experimentation, it is relatively easy to have the same number of subjects per cell (although even "the best-laid plans . . ."). By contrast, survey respondents seldom are selected so as to have the same number of cases per cell. When the number of cases per cell differs widely in a multiple-factor ANOVA design, there are serious problems deciding how to allocate degrees of freedom among main effects, interaction effects, and error. The result is that the power of the F test may be somewhat eroded by uneven cell frequencies.

A third problem of expanded ANOVA models is the rapidly increasing number of interactions and how to interpret them. Suppose we have three factors and find that the three-way interaction and one of the two-way interactions are significant but that the two other two-way interactions are not. Although we can state formally what those tests mean, it may be hard to decide theoretically just what those patterns of interaction mean. The more complex our design, the more likely it will be that translating the results back to the level of theory will be far from simple.

For reasons of cost as well as clarity, then, it often is more prudent to keep research designs relatively simple. This should not discourage you from thinking of more complex designs. It should, however, remind you that simplicity and elegance are the hallmarks of clear theory and definitive research. If you really think that a great number of factors is needed to explain some phenomenon, then perhaps you need to clarify your theory before gathering data to test it.

6 Repeated Measures Analysis of Variance

Up to now, we have discussed ANOVA models that assume that each subject is measured only once. That is the most common type of research design, but it may not be the most efficient. As with any research design, variation due to factors not built into the experimental design gets treated as error, but suppose we can explain some of that variation. Then it will help our tests of theoretically important hypotheses to incorporate the explanatory factor into the research design. The result will be a smaller unexplained sum of squares, hence a smaller within estimate of variance (one-way ANOVA) or error estimate of variance (n-way ANOVA). That in turn will enhance both the F ratios and the related effect sizes for the test of the central hypotheses of the study. One way in which to account for some of the variation across subjects is a repeated measures design.

Consider the stooge experiment once more. Suppose that instead of having different groups experience the different treatments, we had each subject experience each of the treatments in turn. Of course, we would want to randomize the order in which the treatments were experienced to be sure that there was no accidental order effect. When it came to analyzing the data, we could look at how each subject's responses varied across treatments and average those *within-subject* but *between-treatment* effects over all subjects. Any variation from subject to subject in overall response tendency would be removed from the data because we only would look at how any given subject differed between treatments.

The idea just expressed is not simple, so let's look at an example. Suppose we run two versions of the same study. Version 1 is a simple one-way ANOVA with two treatments: Four subjects experience Treatment A and four experience Treatment B. In version 2, however, we have just four subjects experience both treatments, varying the

Exhibit 6.1

Two Versions of a Simple One-Way Experiment

	Separate Samples					Repeated Measures		

Separate Samples

Treatment			
A		B	
Subject	Score	Subject	Score
1	5	5	11
2	2	6	8
3	4	7	10
4	1	8	7

Repeated Measures

	Treatment		Within-Subject Mean
Subject	A	B	
	Score	Score	
1	5	11	8
2	2	8	5
3	4	10	7
4	1	7	4

order in which the treatments are administered. Each experiment generates eight subject scores, like those shown in Exhibit 6.1.

The two examples have identical sets of scores, and so we know that SS_T will be the same in the two studies. It equals 92. Also, the sum of squares attributable to difference between the treatments will be the same: $SS_B = 20$. But notice that, in the repeated measures design, we have discovered something important about the individual subjects. Subject 1 responds with the highest scores to both treatments, Subject 4 responds with the lowest scores, and so on. In short, *on the average, the subjects vary in how they respond to this type of experiment.*

In the separate sample version, there is no way to sort out the variation from subject to subject in how they react. Consequently, variation across subjects is treated as part of the overall error, or SS_W. In the repeated measures version, the within-subject means show us that some of the overall sum of squares is attributable to differences among subjects. We could calculate a within-subject sum of squares separate from the error sum of squares. Actually, for this overly simple example, we would find that the entire SS_W would be attributable to differences among the subjects. That is, all variation in the data is due either to the treatments or to the subjects' differential response tendencies. There is no unexplained or error variance in the entire experiment. You will not find such a convenient result in real research, but a repeated measures design may well show that a sizable portion of what would have been treated as error is in fact due to differences in how subjects respond to experiments in general.

Three Types of Repeated Measures Designs

The approach just described is one version of a repeated measures design. If each subject experiences all treatments, then the treatment effects can be compared to an error estimate that is free of variation across subjects. There can be some major difficulties with repeated measures designs, however, and so do not assume that this approach is a panacea for all experimentation. We will consider possible problems with this type of design later.

A second possibility would be to have each subject experience exactly the same situation several times, such as trying a particular task T different times. If there are learning effects from the repetition, then it will be possible to estimate the curve of learning across successive trials. If there are no learning effects, then the average response for each subject represents an estimate in which within-subject variation (e.g., unreliability) has been removed. Either way, this approach is also a repeated measures problem. Rather than comparing across treatments, it compares across experience. Again, there are potential problems, which will be dealt with later.

For a third type of repeated measures design, suppose we have each subject experience a standardized progression of some stimulus. Asch's (1951) classic experiments on the influence of groups on individual judgments demonstrated a sizable chance that someone faced with unanimous but *incorrect* judgmental statements from others will concur with those incorrect judgments, at least publicly. The task involved making simple visual judgments. Each person in the group announced aloud his or her judgment, and intentionally incorrect judgments were rendered by confederates of the experiment. (See? Using stooges has a long history in experimental work.) Having one other naive subject in the group greatly reduced the probability of incorrect judgments. More than one other naive subject nearly eliminated the group effect. Of course, each subject experienced only one experimental condition.

Suppose the same subject had participated in five different groups, all having six other members, and that the number of naive subjects in any group varied from zero to four, with the rest of the group being confederates of the experiment. The set of other members experienced by each subject would look like the following:

0 naive   6 confederates
1 naive   5 confederates
2 naive   4 confederates
3 naive   3 confederates
4 naive   2 confederates

Clearly, contamination of experience across the six different group experiences could be a problem with this design, and order of experience might be as well. If those problems could be controlled (yes, that is a huge *if*), then the data would allow us to calculate a curve of the probability of being influenced as a function of the size of the faction giving incorrect responses. Comparisons would be across treatments within each subject's response record, making each subject his or her own control. The result would be a more precise statement of the effect of group opinion on one's public response. This type of design typically is used for problems involving systematic progression of stimuli such as different dosages of a drug. Keep in mind that there may well be problems with these designs. We will discuss them in some detail at the end of the chapter.

A Repeated Measures Version of the Stooge Experiment

Obviously, the stooge study was not run as a repeated measures design, but let's suppose that it had been. The original data are arranged in Exhibit 6.2 as if 12 subjects each had experienced all four treatments rather than 48 subjects each experiencing one treatment.

It would be very unlikely, of course, but assume that the highest response in Treatment 1 came from the same subject who gave the highest response in Treatment 2, who also gave the highest response in Treatment 3, and so forth, just like the simple example in Exhibit 6.1. In other words, a major source of within-treatment variation would be differences among the subjects in how they tended to respond to such a situation. Such a convenient fiction will make it easier to see how important a repeated measures design could be for explaining observed variation in the data.

Exhibit 6.2

Repeated Measures Version of Stooge Data

		Treatment			
Subject	Con-Neat	Con-Slop	Hes-Neat	Hes-Slop	Sum
1	1.50	1.50	1.00	0.50	4.50
2	1.25	1.25	0.50	0.27	3.27
3	1.00	1.00	0.50	0.00	2.50
4	0.75	1.00	0.00	0.00	1.75
5	0.39	0.50	0.00	0.00	0.89
6	0.00	0.00	0.00	0.00	0.00
7	0.00	0.00	0.00	−0.34	−0.34
8	0.00	0.00	0.00	−0.40	−0.40
9	0.00	0.00	−0.08	−0.89	−0.97
10	0.00	0.00	−0.50	−1.00	−1.50
11	0.00	0.00	−1.00	−1.00	−2.00
12	−0.25	−0.10	−1.00	−1.27	−2.62
Sum	4.64	5.15	−0.58	−4.13	5.08

Calculating ANOVA

The calculations for this repeated measures problem are essentially the same as those for a two-way ANOVA. Again, we have to assume that there is no carryover of effect from one treatment experience to another and also that there is no effect of the order in which the treatments were experienced.

As before, we will need SS_T, the total sum of squares. We also need a between-treatments sum of squares. For the way in which the data are arrayed in Exhibit 6.1, the columns are the different treatments, so SS_{Treat} will be just like the column sum of squares in a two-way ANOVA. The equivalent for the rows of Exhibit 6.2 represents a within-subject sum of squares: SS_{Subj}. Recall from Chapter 5 that a two-way ANOVA generates three sources of explanation: columns, rows, and row × column interaction. There is also a separate error sum of squares calculated by variation within each cell around the cell means.

For the repeated measures design, we also have three sources of explanation: treatments, subjects, and what sometimes is called subject × treatment interaction (see Edwards, 1979). With only one case per subject × treatment cell, however, we cannot calculate an interaction sum of squares that is separate from a within-cell or error sum of squares. The columns represent how subjects in general respond to a particular treatment, and the rows represent how a given subject responds to this type of experiment. What would be thought of as the row × column interaction represents the unique and presumably random variation of individual responses to particular treatments as deviations from what would be expected if each response were a precise and additive consequence of subject predilection and treatment effect. This would-be interaction term, then, generates the error sum of squares for this repeated measures model.

To calculate the needed sums of squares "from scratch," obtain SS_T in the usual way. Compute ΣY^2, the sum of squared observations over all cases and treatments. Compute $(\Sigma Y)^2$, the square of the sum of all observations. Divide $(\Sigma Y)^2$ by the total number of observations and subtract the result from ΣY^2. That is,

$$SS_T = \sum_i \sum_c Y_{ic}^2 - \frac{\left(\sum_i \sum_c Y_{ij}\right)^2}{n_c C}.$$

Note that we assume that there are $i = 1 .. n$ subjects and $c = 1 .. C$ treatments, with each subject experiencing each treatment once. We will not need to do those calculations, however, because the result necessarily will be the same value we obtained originally in Chapter 3 and again in Chapter 5: $SS_T = 19.8844$.

Calculating SS_{Treat} will again follow the usual routine. Take ΣY for each treatment, square it, and divide that square by the number of observations in that treatment. Add those results over all treatments. Then subtract the same "correction" term used in calculating SS_T:

$$SS_{Treat} = \sum_c \frac{\left(\sum_i Y_{ic}\right)^2}{n_c} - \frac{\left(\sum_i \sum_c Y_{ic}\right)^2}{n_c C}.$$

Because n_c, the number of cases in a given column, is the same for all c, it is easier to square each treatment total, add those squares, and divide the sum by n_c. Using the treatment and total sums from Exhibit 6.2, the calculations for SS_{Treat} are as shown in the following. Note that this result is the same value obtained in Chapter 3 as SS_B.

$$\sum_c \frac{\left(\sum_i Y_{ic}\right)^2}{n_c} = \frac{[(4.64)^2 + (-0.58)^2 + (5.15)^2 + (-4.13)^2]}{12} = 5.4538.$$

$$\frac{\left(\sum_i \sum_c Y_{ic}\right)^2}{48} = .5376.$$

$$SS_{Treat} = 5.4538 - .5376 = 4.9162.$$

You can calculate SS_{Subj} just like a row sum of squares for two-way ANOVA. Square each row total (i.e., subject total) and divide it by C, the number of columns, or the number of treatments. Add those amounts over all subjects and subtract the same correction term used for SS_T and SS_{Treat}. Because C is constant over all subjects, we might as well just add the squared subject totals and then divide the sum by C. That gives

$$\sum_i \frac{\left(\sum_c Y_{ic}\right)^2}{C} = [(4.50)^2 + (3.27)^2 + (2.50)^2 + (1.75)^2$$

$$+ (0.89)^2 + 0^2 + (-.34)^2 + (-.40)^2 + (-.97)^2$$

$$+ (-1.50)^2 + (-2.00)^2 + (-2.62)^2] / 4 = 13.8446$$

$$SS_{Subj} = 13.8446 - .5376 = 13.3070 .$$

We now have SS_T, SS_{Treat}, and SS_{Subj}. As already noted, the remaining sum of squares, which in a typical two-way model would be divided between $SS_{Interaction}$ and SS_{Error}, cannot be so divided here. It will be used as the error sum of squares for the F tests.

$$SS_E = SS_T - SS_{Treat} - SS_{Subj} = 19.8844 - 4.9162 - 13.3070 = 1.6612.$$

The only remaining consideration for constructing an F test for the treatment effects is calculating appropriate degrees of freedom. For C treatments, we have $C - 1$ degrees of freedom: $df_{Treat} = 4 - 1 = 3$. For error, we have $(n - 1)(C - 1)$ degrees of freedom (parallel to the interaction degrees of freedom from two-way ANOVA), where n is the number of subjects and C is the number of treatments. Therefore, $df_E = (11)(3) = 33$.

Exhibit 6.3

F Test for Treatment Effects

Source	SS	df	MS	F
Subjects	13.3070	11		
Treatments	4.9162	3	1.6387	32.5785
Error	1.6612	33	0.0503	
Total	19.8844	47		

With 48 observations, $df_{Total} = 47$. We have just accounted for 36 of them (3 + 33). The remaining 11 are attributable to subjects: $df_{Subj} = n - 1 = 11$. Contrary to a two-way ANOVA, the only relevant test in this version of a repeated measures design is for treatments. That is, the equivalent null hypothesis for subjects would be that all subjects have the same mean response to the experiment, and this tells us nothing about the focal concern with the treatment effects. Exhibit 6.3 shows the F table.

Obviously, there is a highly significant treatment effect after controlling for the within-subject variation. This is a much larger F than was obtained in earlier analyses of the same data, even though the treatment sum of squares is the same as before. Of course, we have created a fictitious data set based on the original data in such a way that the maximum possible amount of variation was within subjects. By controlling the within-subject sum of squares, we have reduced the error sum of squares a great deal, making the error mean square only about one seventh of what it was in the one-way analysis of Chapter 3. Consequently, our F here is about seven times larger. The importance of a repeated measures design, therefore, should be obvious: If a large part of variation is between subjects in how they react to the experimental situation in general, and if repeated measures methods can be used without confounding the data, then a much more powerful test of the main treatment hypothesis is possible.

Using SPSS for Repeated Measures Tests

Neither ONEWAY nor the ANOVA routine in SPSS accommodates repeated measures designs. However, MANOVA (which stands for multiple analysis of variance) in SPSS contains provisions for such an analysis. There are many options in MANOVA—too many to discuss here. We will consider the simplest approach to solving the problem.

Assuming that the data in Exhibit 6.1 are in a file called Rep-Meas.dat, and approaching SPSS from scratch rather than from a system file, we need only the following commands:

```
DATA LIST FILE='RepMeas.dat' FREE
/NeatCon NeatHes SlopCon SlopHes.
MANOVA NeatCon NeatHes SlopCon SlopHes
/WSfactors=Treatmnt (4).
```

This very simple command file contains two parts.

The first two lines call up the data file and label the four treatment variables (four entries for each case). The second two lines specify the MANOVA. It is essential to repeat the four treatment labels on the MANOVA command even though they were just listed in the DATA LIST command. Further, it is essential to include the WSfactors statement because it tells SPSS that this is a within-subjects, or repeated measures, design. The statement WSfactors= Treatment (4) says that the first four variables listed in the MANOVA command are the four repeated measures. Because only four variables were listed, no further information is needed.

Exhibit 6.4 shows the Tests Involving 'TREATMENT' Within-Subject Effect portion of SPSS printout, which is the portion directly relevant to our hypothesis. There are several other parts of the total printout that will not be presented here because they deal with technical questions beyond the scope of this brief discussion.

Notice that there is no total sum of squares shown here and that SS_{Subj} from Exhibit 6.3 does not appear. The other two sums of squares are present, labeled WITHIN CELLS (our SS_E) and TREATMNT (our SS_{Treat}). They agree with our earlier calculations within the two-place rounding error used by SPSS. Similarly, the degrees of freedom agree and the calculated F differs only in the second decimal place, apparently due to rounding differences between our calculations and those of SPSS.

As is evident from the simple SPSS program and the ease of interpreting results, analyzing a single-factor repeated measures design is no problem in SPSS. Things can get a lot more complicated if there are two or more factors and/or one or more covariates, but

Exhibit 6.4

SPSS Results for a Repeated Measures Problem

```
Tests involving 'TREATMNT' Within-Subject Effect

AVERAGED Tests of Significance for MEAS.1 using UNIQUE sums of squares
Source of Variation        SS       DF       MS       F   Sig of F

WITHIN CELLS             1.66      33      .05
TREATMNT                 4.92       3     1.64    32.55      .000
```

the principles discussed earlier are the same. It is also possible to generate treatment contrasts just as was done in Chapter 3. Once again, if the potential problems of repeated measures designs can be overcome, then they provide a powerful way in which to rule out between-subject variation, resulting in sharper tests of hypotheses.

Repeated Measures in Learning Experiments

The stooge data will not help us explore the second type of repeated measures design described earlier in this chapter, but you probably have had too much of those data by now anyway. The type of design we turn to now is one in which each case experiences the same stimulus a number of times. The focus typically is on the curve over time in learning or response time, task efficiency, or some other aspect of observable behavior. The intent of such a design is not to test whether different treatments have different effects but rather to test whether successive exposure to a stimulus generates systematic change in response.

A Group Learning Example

Suppose a corporation decides to create a task force to address a particular type of recurrent question such as deciding whether suggestions from the worker suggestion boxes are worth passing along for serious consideration. The chief executive officer, or CEO, appoints a leader and a group and gives them their charge in general terms. If the first meeting takes a long time and does not seem to get much done, does that mean the task force idea is a bad one? Not necessarily.

A great deal of research on the dynamics of social groups has resulted in a variety of theories about how groups form and develop over time. A common theme in most group developmental models is that the first phase or stage is likely to be characterized by hesitance, politeness, and wariness (see, e.g., Bion, 1959; Parsons, 1961; Tuckerman & Jensen, 1977; Wheelan, 1994). The members are not sure what to expect, how they will fit in, whether to trust the leader, and so forth. In this stage, there is likely to be little disagreement, but there will not be much accomplished either.

As they gain confidence in the setting, the members are likely to start expressing differences of opinion. This generates debates, possible splitting into factions, and possible challenges to the leader. Task accomplishments remain low because energy is going into sorting out rules, roles, and relationships. Eventually, assuming the group gets past this set of problems, members begin to agree on the group's functioning and their place in it. Finally, it will be possible to attend to objective tasks. Such a work phase is likely to last a long time if the group continues.

Now, suppose the CEO is concerned about the curve of productivity of such groups. Does she have reason to believe that a slow start is not a matter of concern? If data on successive meetings of such a task force were available, how could we analyze them to determine the curve of productivity? Let's design an experiment.

First, this time our case will be a *group*, not an individual. Second, we will need to study several groups because each group is to some extent unique even though we assume that groups go through comparable developmental stages. Third, we will need to have each group meet several times and face a new set of decisions each time. Finally, we need some index of productivity such as the number of decisions made per meeting. The decisions should be comparable in difficulty so that the only question is the successive levels of productivity.

Clearly, this is a repeated measures example, where the successive productivity indexes for a given group constitute the repeated measures. Note that there is a major contrast with the earlier example of each subject in the stooge experiment experiencing all four treatments. Now there will be no treatment variations, just a repetition of meetings doing essentially the same task. For convenience,

Exhibit 6.5

Group Productivity Over Successive Meetings

Group	First Meeting	Second Meeting	Third Meeting	Fourth Meeting	Sum
1	0	1	4	9	14
2	1	1	3	7	12
3	1	2	5	10	18
4	2	3	4	9	18
5	0	1	3	6	10
6	1	2	5	12	20
7	1	1	4	7	13
8	0	1	2	6	9
Sum	6	12	30	66	114

assume that we have eight groups, each group meets four times, and each time the group is presented with a new set of, say, 10 possible decisions to make. Again to minimize any possible order effect, the order of presentation of problems for decision could be randomized.

The data set might look like that shown in Exhibit 6.5. Of course, these are fictitious data for illustration only. The entries represent how many decisions are made by each group in each of the four meetings. It is clear from Exhibit 6.5 that the number of decisions made increases over successive meetings. A graph of the average number of decisions made for each of the four meetings is shown in Exhibit 6.6. Not only does productivity increase over time, it seems to accelerate.

Calculating Effects

First, let's do the same repeated measures ANOVA we have done previously, just to be sure that there is significant change in productivity over time. After all, if there was no significant difference, then more elaborate analysis would be pointless. The relevant sums of squares are shown in Exhibit 6.7, with the F test for the effect of meetings shown in Exhibit 6.8. There is a highly significant effect of number of meetings, just as we thought would be the case. The more interesting problem, however, is the trend of productivity over successive meetings.

Obviously, there is a highly significant effect of time (meetings), but how can we analyze these data so as to determine the pattern of

Exhibit 6.6

Curve of Productivity Over Meetings

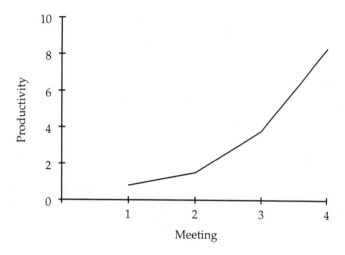

Exhibit 6.7

Sums of Squares for Group Productivity Data

$$SS_T = 0^2 + 1^2 + 1^2 + \ldots + 6^2 - \frac{114^2}{32} = 319.875$$

$$SS_{mtg} = \frac{6^2}{8} + \frac{12^2}{8} + \frac{30^2}{8} + \frac{66^2}{8} - \frac{114^2}{32} = 273.375$$

$$SS_{gps} = \frac{14^2}{4} + \frac{12^2}{4} + \ldots + \frac{9^2}{4} - \frac{114^2}{32} = 28.375$$

$$SS_E = SS_T - SS_{mtg} - SS_{gps} = 18.125$$

change over successive meetings? It no longer is sufficient to ask whether the mean productivity differs among meetings 1, 2, 3, and 4. The interesting question is whether there is a particular *curve* of productivity. That question is best answered in one of two ways. The most precise way theoretically would be to fit a specific mathematical equation such as one for exponential growth. However, that requires theoretical and mathematical sophistication as well as fitting techniques not found in most statistical packages. We will try a more general approach instead.

Exhibit 6.8

Test for Effect of Meetings

Source	SS	df	MS	F
Subjects	28.375	7		
Meetings	273.375	3	91.125	105.591
Error	18.125	21	0.863	
Total	319.875	31		

The more general approach is to fit a polynomial equation to the data. There are two advantages: It does not require theorizing about the precise form of the curve, and it can be readily accomplished by SPSS. The form of the equation is $Y = a + b_1X + b_2X^2 + \ldots + b_kX^k + e$. There can be at most $k - 1$ powers in the equation when there are k values of the independent variable. In our group productivity example, there were four meetings. Therefore, we can have only the first, second, and third power terms in the equation.

What do these terms mean? The first power of X generates a standard linear component of the predicted Y: Y will change a constant amount as X increases one unit. The second power generates a quadratic component, which means the curve will have one major bend in it. Each higher power contributes a component that contains one more bend in the curve. A cubic component has two bends, a quartic component has three, and so forth. In principle, you can fit any kind of curve by throwing in enough higher powers.

When a lot of higher powers are used and found to be significant, it gets very difficult to interpret the results. With only three powers, however, we can easily sort out the meaning of any significant components. If b_1 is positive, then the curve of Y generally increases over the values of X, whereas a negative b_1 would imply a general decrease of Y over the values of X. If b_2 is positive, then the curve bends upward, or accelerates. If b_2 is negative, then the curve bends downward, such as starting off with a strong gain that diminishes over successive meetings. If b_3 is significant, then the direction of bend changes. For example, an initially accelerating curve (upward bending) might start to taper off or even decline in later meetings (downward bend).

There are two problems for analyzing our data, then. The first is to figure out how to do the calculations for estimating the b coeffi-

Exhibit 6.9

Calculations Using Orthogonal Polynomial Coefficients

	Meeting				ΣX^2	$\Sigma X\overline{Y}$	$\dfrac{n(\Sigma\, X\overline{Y})^2}{\Sigma X^2}$
	1	2	3	4			
$\overline{Y}$	.75	1.5	3.75	8.25			
X1	−3	−1	1	3	20	24.75	245.025
X2	1	−1	−1	1	4	3.75	28.125
X3	−1	3	−3	1	20	.75	.225
							273.375

cients. The second is to test those estimates to see which, if any, are significant. As always, we can do the calculations by hand or by SPSS. Both approaches will be illustrated.

The easiest approach for doing the computations ourselves is to use coefficients for creating orthogonal polynomials. Working out the logic behind these coefficients takes more space than is available here, and so we will simply use values from a table provided by Edwards (1979, p. 208, Table III). The values are appropriate only if two conditions are satisfied. We must have an equal number of observations for each treatment (or successive meeting, for this example), and we have this because the same number of groups is observed for all successive meetings. Also, successive treatments must involve equally spaced increments of whatever the treatment involves. In this case, we simply added one more meeting each time, and so we have equally spaced stimuli. For estimating orthogonal polynomial coefficients in cases of unequal ns or unequal stimulus intervals, Edwards recommends Gaito (1965).

Exhibit 6.9 has two parts. The left side shows the mean value of the dependent variable, Y (number of problems solved), and the orthogonal polynomial from Edwards for linear (X1), quadratic (X2), and cubic (X3) effects in each of four columns, one for each meeting. The right-hand portion shows the sums of squares and products. We will go over the necessary computations. First, however, notice that the total under the last column, 273.375, is the same value we found earlier for the sum of squares for meetings. For this analysis, we are interested in partitioning that SS_{mtg} into its linear, quadratic, and cubic components.

Each of the row entries in that last column contains those sums of squares attributable to each of the three components of the curve. Each sum of squares has 1 df, and together they add up to the 3 df for SS_{mtg}. Calculations for these sums really are quite simple. Start with the X1 row. To get the entry in the ΣX^2 column, simply square each of the X1 values in the four meeting columns and add them up:

$$(-3)^2 + (-1)^2 + 1^2 + 3^2 = 20.$$

Do the same for the X2 and X3 rows and you should get ΣX^2 values of 4 and 20, respectively.

To get the entries in the next column, multiply each X value by its corresponding $\overline{Y}$ value for that column and add over columns:

$$(-3)(.75) + (-1)(1.5) + (1)(3.75) + (3)(8.25) = 24.75$$

for the X1 row. The same approach will yield the entries shown for the X2 and X3 rows. Finally, to get the last column, square the sum of products just obtained, multiply by the number of cases, and divide by the ΣX^2 term. Again for the X1 row, square 24.75, multiply by 8 for the number of groups, and divide by 20:

$$\frac{n \left(\sum X \overline{Y} \right)^2}{\sum X^2} = \frac{8 (24.75)^2}{20} = 245.025.$$

Follow the same procedure for the other rows.

The F tests for these effects will all use MS_E from the ANOVA shown in Exhibit 6.8: $MS_E = .863$ with 21 df. The three component sums of squares come from the calculations for Exhibit 6.9. As noted before, each component sum of squares has 1 df. Therefore, the tests are as follows:

$$F_{Linear} = 245.025/.863 = 283.922$$

$$F_{Quadratic} = 28.125/.863 = 32.590$$

$$F_{Cubic} = .225/.863 = .261.$$

For 1 and 21 df, $F_{.01} = 8.02$. Obviously, the linear and quadratic effects are significant, as our visual inspection suggested would be the case. The cubic effect is trivial, and this agrees with the fact that there was no double bend in the curve.

Our CEO could conclude, therefore, that not getting much done in the first meeting does not imply that the groups are useless. Rather, they get better as time goes on, even accelerating in their

Exhibit 6.10

SPSS Program for the Group Productivity Problem

```
DATA LIST FILE 'd:\spss\data\rep-meet.dat' FREE
  /mtg1  mtg2  mtg3  mtg4.
manova mtg1 mtg2 mtg3 mtg4
  /wsfactors=meeting (4)
  /contrast(meeting)=polynomial
  /rename=const linear quadratc cubic
  /wsdesign
  /print=parameters(estim)
  /design.
```

productivity. One note of warning for this example: Clearly, there would come a time when productivity would not continue to climb. In fact, it is not uncommon for groups to decline in productivity after an initial growth period.

Using SPSS for the Group Productivity Problem

The calculations just demonstrated are not difficult, but it is very simple to get all necessary results from the SPSS MANOVA program. Assume we have an appropriate data file called ‘REP-MEET.DAT’ and it happens to be in drive D, directory SPSS, subdirectory Data. The file lists one row for each group, and each row contains the number of decisions made by that group for each of the meetings in order. There is no problem using subdirectory specification in SPSS's DATA LIST command. A complete program for the group productivity problem is shown Exhibit 6.10.

Note that variable labels are used to keep track of the meetings: mtg1, mtg2, mtg3, and mtg4. These labels need to be repeated on the MANOVA line. The WSFACTORS=MEETING(4) command is necessary, as already noted, but several new lines are added. In particular, CONTRAST(MEETING)=POLYNOMIAL specifies orthogonal polynomials, and the next line provides names for the components. The first component, named CONST, is simply the intercept of the regression equation, and its test asks whether the overall average productivity is zero. The other three component names are obvious from our prior analysis. Incidentally, the DESIGN command

Exhibit 6.11

_F_ Test for the Constant Term

```
Tests of Significance for CONST using UNIQUE sums of squares.
Source of Variation        SS      DF      MS        F    Sig of F

WITHIN CELLS            28.38       7     4.05
CONSTANT               406.13       1   406.13    100.19      .000


- - - - - - - - - -
Estimates for CONST
CONSTANT

 Parameter    Coeff.   Std. Err.  t-Value   Sig. t  Lower -95% CL- Upper
    1     7.12500000    .71183   10.00947    .000    5.44180     8.80820
```

at the end is always necessary, even if no special design requests are desired.

A test for the constant is shown in Exhibit 6.11. Because $p = .000$, we reject the null hypothesis that the constant equals zero. There is a nonzero average level of productivity. (The boss ought to heave a sigh of relief over that, shouldn't she?)

The three tests for the components of the curve are shown in Exhibit 6.12. They agree completely with the calculations already done. Both the linear and quadratic components are significant, whereas the cubic component is not. Incidentally, you can use either the estimated probability or the confidence limits to check each hypothesis. If the confidence limits do not include zero, then there is reason to reject the null hypothesis.

Note that all the sums of squares that we calculated previously can be found in Exhibits 6.11 and 6.12. The sum of squares for CONSTANT in Exhibit 6.11 is 406.13. If you check Exhibit 6.7, you can see that the residual term, or correction factor, for SS_T, SS_{mtg}, and SS_{gps} is $(114)^2/32$, or 406.125, which SPSS rounds to 406.13. That term has to do with deviation of the overall mean from zero. The value for SS_{gps} in Exhibit 6.7, once 406.13 is subtracted out, is 28.375 (rounded to 28.38 by SPSS). Therefore, the calculations shown by SPSS in Exhibit 6.11 divide the total variation of the data into the sum of squares of the grand mean around zero versus the sum of squares within the groups. The latter constitutes "error" for the sake of asking whether the overall mean deviates from zero.

Exhibit 6.12

Tests for the Three Curve Components

```
AVERAGED Tests of Significance for MTG using UNIQUE sums of squares
Source of Variation          SS        DF       MS        F    Sig of F

WITHIN CELLS               18.13       21      .86
MEETING                   273.37        3    91.12    105.58      .000

Estimates for LINEAR
MEETING
 Parameter      Coeff.    Std. Err.   t-Value   Sig. t  Lower -95% CL- Upper
      1      5.53426824    .50134    11.03901    .000     4.34880     6.71974

Estimates for QUADRATC
MEETING
 Parameter      Coeff.    Std. Err.   t-Value   Sig. t  Lower -95% CL- Upper
      1      1.87500000    .20594     9.10465    .000     1.38803     2.36197

Estimates for CUBIC
MEETING
 Parameter      Coeff.    Std. Err.   t-Value   Sig. t  Lower -95% CL- Upper
      1       .167705098   .17295      .96969    .365    -.24125      .57666
```

Do not be confused by SPSS using the term WITHIN CELLS for two different results in the two exhibits. Exhibit 6.11 concerns only the question of whether, on the average, group productivity is zero. Any sum of squares considered "error" for the test under consideration gets labeled WITHIN CELLS. For Exhibit 6.12, the only "error" is the variation not explained by meetings or groups, and that is our SS_E of 18.125 rounded to two places. That leaves the 273.375 (or 273.37) sum of squares for meetings to be partitioned among the linear, quadratic, and cubic components.

The SPSS printout in Exhibit 6.12 provides four tests. The general test is whether successive meetings have significant effects. It is shown as an F test using the two sums of squares just discussed and generates an F of 105.58 with a significance of .000. Within rounding error, that duplicates our finding in Exhibit 6.8 that there is a significant effect of meetings over time.

Because the remainder of the tests all involve only 1 df, they are shown as t tests rather than as F tests. Remember that F with 1 in the numerator is equal to t^2. The results again duplicate our earlier findings: a very significant linear effect, a less strong but still significant quadratic effect, and a nonsignificant cubic effect. According to these data, and using the formal logic of hypothesis testing, the boss would be warranted in concluding not only that group productivity does increase over meetings but that it accelerates.

A Third Version of Repeated Measures

At the beginning of this chapter, three different versions of repeated measures designs were suggested. We have looked at two in detail. The third involved each subject experiencing a standard progression of a stimulus such as graded dosages of a drug or progressively louder sounds. If the gradations of stimulus are equal, such as dosages of 5, 10, 15, and 20, then the procedures just used will be correct. You can solve for overall effects and for components of the curve of response over the stimulus progression in exactly the same manner. When the stimulus intervals are not equal, the problem is more complicated than we have space to explore in detail here. Fortunately, a very minor addition to the SPSS MANOVA program will accommodate unequal stimulus intervals.

Suppose that, instead of the first 4 group meetings, the data we have been using came from the 1st, 2nd, 5th, and 10th meetings. All that we need to do with the program shown in Exhibit 6.10 is modify the CONTRAST command:

```
CONTRAST(MEETING)=POLYNOMIAL(1,2,5,10).
```

The parentheses after the word POLYNOMIAL now let SPSS know what the relative spacing of stimuli are (i.e., those meetings for which we have data). Most of what we already have examined will remain unchanged because the values of the dependent variable are just what they were before. However, the components of the curve describing change in productivity over successive meetings should be quite different.

SPSS results using the new spacing are instructive. The linear trend remains significant across the number of decisions made, and the cubic effect remains negligible as before. However, the quadratic effect has become nonsignificant as well. With both the second and third components nil, we must have a straight line. In fact, if you do a quick plot of the mean number of decisions for each successive meeting number, using meetings spaced at 1, 2, 5, and 10, you will find an almost perfectly straight line of increasing productivity. If the data had actually come from meetings 1, 2, 5, and 10 but we had left that information out of the POLYNOMIAL command, then we would have incorrectly concluded that there was acceleration in productivity over time.

Assumptions of Repeated Measures Designs

There are several assumptions underlying the statistical procedures we have been examining. Properly, they should be checked before calculating and interpreting the significance tests. The usual assumptions of normality and independence obtain, of course, but as noted earlier, there is an additional assumption. The examples used here have involved only one dependent variable and one design factor: a simplest type of design. In effect, the repeated measures computations create new variables: a *linear* variable, a *quadratic* variable, and so on. For the F test to retain its power, the variances of all transformed variables should be equal and their covariances should equal zero. The equal variance requirement echoes our old friend homoscedasticity. Remember that a covariance is just the numerator of a correlation coefficient, so this second criterion in effect says that the transformed variables should be uncorrelated.

If you calculated all the variances and covariances for the variables, then you could create what is called a *variance-covariance matrix*. Such a matrix is just a table with one row and one column for each variable, listed in the same order. Each entry in the main diagonal of the matrix (i.e., same variable for the row and the column) would be a variance, and each of the other entries (off-diagonal) would be a covariance between variables for the particular row and column for that cell of the matrix. To satisfy the joint conditions just noted, the main diagonal entries all should be within sampling variation of the same population value, and the off-diagonal entries should be within sampling variation of zero.

SPSS can calculate that matrix and make appropriate tests of the assumptions. When sample size is large, a test called the *Mauchly test of sphericity* calculates the likelihood of the observed data under the assumptions of constant diagonal and zero off-diagonal elements in the population variance-covariance matrix. When n is small, the test is not very powerful (see Norusis, 1988b, p. B-162). If the Mauchly test fails, which is the case when the calculated significance falls below α, then it may be desirable to make some downward adjustments in both the numerator and the denominator degrees of freedom for F tests or in just the denominator degrees of freedom for t tests. What such an adjustment in degrees of freedom does, in effect, is to require stronger results to reject a null hypothesis at the specified α level. The threat to the F or t test due to violation of the assumptions is offset by treating the data as if there were fewer degrees of freedom.

Fortunately, SPSS provides the Mauchly test. For all the tests in this chapter, the "sphericity" assumption is a bit of a problem. The data on group productivity, for example, generate a significance of .01 for the Mauchly test. Because that is below α, we should properly make some adjustment to preserve our confidence in the separate tests. Again fortunately, SPSS also provides some estimates of a coefficient called *epsilon*, which can be used to adjust degrees of freedom. Two such estimates are provided: one called the Greenhouse-Geisser estimate, which tends to be very conservative, and another called the Huynh-Feldt estimate, which is less so.

For the group productivity data, the Huynh-Feldt estimate of epsilon was .50. So what does one do with epsilon? For the t tests of the curve components in the group problem-solving example provided in Exhibit 6.12, there were 21 df (see Exhibit 6.8). Use the .50 value of epsilon as a multiple for the degrees of freedom: $(.50)(21) =$ 10.5. A significant t for 10 df is 2.76 for a one-tailed test with $\alpha = .01$ compared to 2.518 for 21 df. Consequently, the calculated values of t for the tests will have to be somewhat larger to reach significance after we use the correction.

Calculated t values for linear, quadratic, and cubic effects were 11.04, 9.10, and .97, respectively. Clearly, the linear and quadratic components still are significant after the adjustment in degrees of freedom. The cubic is not significant, but it was not earlier either. For the version assuming meetings 1, 2, 5, and 10, the t values were 11.04 (not affected by change in the horizontal scale), .136, and .779, respectively. The linear effect remains significant despite the correction.

In these data, then, the test for sphericity, the added assumption required by the repeated measures design, has demonstrated some problem with the assumption. However, making an adjustment in degrees of freedom based on the epsilon factor recommended by the Huynh-Feldt procedure has not altered our conclusions. You may not always be so lucky, however. Sometimes apparently significant results can be the consequence of a major violation of assumptions.

If there are one or more design factors in the experiment, then there is a variance-covariance matrix for transformed variables for each level of the factor (e.g., for male groups vs. female groups). In that case, the variance-covariance matrices for all levels of the factor must be equal. Again, that can be tested automatically in SPSS MANOVA.

The Other Assumptions

The obvious advantage of a repeated measures design is that each case (individual subject, group, or whatever) is used as its own control. That advantage is bought at the price of being sure (a) that the repeated measures are independent and (b) that they have the same variance for all treatments. Remember that the F test assumes that residuals, the basis for SS_E, are independent and normally distributed. To generate a single estimate of SS_E by pooling the within-group (or within-treatment) sums of squares and degrees of freedom, each group must have the same within-group error variance. If these criteria are met for all treatments, then the covariances of error among treatments will be zero and the variances will be equal, satisfying the sphericity criterion discussed before.

What might violate the independence assumption? Consider the type of experiment in which each subject experiences a full range of treatments. One frequent problem for research on people is that each experience may contaminate future experiences. In the case of the repeated measures version of the stooge study, would having to play the game four times have a baseline effect, a learning effect, or a boredom effect independent of the stooge role effect? If any of these effects should arise, then a statistical design assuming independence could be inappropriate.

Suppose that we had each subject exposed to the same order of stooge roles, starting with the neat/confident stooge. That experience might well set a baseline for future responses to other stooge roles. If it affected only the mean response, then it would not violate the independence of error assumptions but it could affect tests of the differences among treatments. However, a baseline effect also could alter the variances, making responses much more variable in one treatment than in another. A typical approach to ruling out such contaminating effects is to randomize the order in which cases experience the different treatments.

More subtle effects could result if there is interaction between adjacent treatments. For example, experiencing the sloppy-confident stooge right after the sloppy-hesitant one might generate quite different response patterns from the reverse order or from other possible pair orderings. If those effects altered the relevant error variance-covariance matrices, then the F test would become less valid. Of course, the tests and adjustments discussed earlier can help correct for such problems.

Regarding the type of design involving successive instances of a given stimulus (meetings, drug dosages, etc.), remember that one question concerns the curve of response. It often is the case that when a process accelerates over time, the variance of response errors around an overall trend increases. That means, for example, that the *variance* of productivity might go up as *average* productivity rose. In fact, that is true for the productivity data. Variances for the four different meetings are .44, .50, .94, and 3.94, respectively. Even though the Mauchly test is not powerful for small Ns, it indicated that these are not plausibly from populations with the same variance.

Summary

Repeated measures designs used with human subject populations can pose serious threats to the validity of the relevant tests. If successive drug dosages are being tested, then how long does it take for the effects of one dosage to wear off so that the next one will not be interacting with the first? Humans learn and remember and may even retain effects of which they are not aware. Sometimes those effects become confounded. This is well documented in survey research, for example, where the ordering of questions can affect responses. Therefore, use of repeated measures methods must be treated with caution.

On the positive side, it is clear that using each case as its own control can greatly increase our ability to detect significant statistical effects. If the people or groups or whatever cases are being studied differ widely in their responses to the same type of situation, then that variation inflates estimates of error and decreases the ability to reject a false null hypothesis. A repeated measures design removes such between-subject variation, leaving a purer estimate of error as the basis for our decisions. That is not the only way in which to control extraneous error, of course.

7 From Statistics to Substantive Theory

This final chapter addresses several ideas that may have been suggested along the way but were not discussed in any detail. There are four main topics here: creating more complex experimental designs, drawing substantive conclusions from sample evidence, testing what we really believe, and distinguishing among statistical, theoretical, and practical significance. Each topic warrants much more than part of a chapter, but the purpose here is to start you thinking beyond the specifics of ANOVA and experimental design.

More Complex Experimental Designs

For simplicity, the designs and related statistical models presented in this book have been quite limited, to just one or two factors. It should be apparent that much more complex designs are possible, although they can require much larger samples. The basic ideas in this section are increasing the number of factors to be manipulated in the experiment, finding ways in which to accommodate these more complex designs without requiring enormous samples, and including what are called *covariates* in the design. All are ways of trying to maximize the theoretical utility of results.

To provide a common thread, let's choose one topic and elaborate on it as we go. Suppose you want to study how people react to propaganda videos, depending on whether they agree or disagree with them. You want an area of strong attitudes, so you decide to choose abortion as the focus. Assume that you have developed a valid, nonreactive way in which to assess reaction, such as videotaping the subjects' faces while they are watching the stimulus video and coding the facial expressions along a relevant dimension such as attentiveness, approval, or anger. The dependent variable, then, is reaction to the video stimulus. (For a variety of interesting analyses regarding abortion attitudes using data from the General Social Survey, see Babbie & Halley, 1994.)

You have two videos that should have opposite effects; one is strongly anti-abortion and the other is strongly pro-abortion. Factor 1, then, is a dichotomy: the anti-abortion video versus the pro-abortion video. Of obvious relevance for the study is the initial attitudes of the subjects. Either you could premeasure your subject population and then select groups of "pros" and "antis," or you could treat initial attitude as something to be measured in advance and statistically manipulated. The latter approach makes initial attitude a covariate, which will be discussed shortly. For now, assume that you opt for selecting the two groups based on initial attitude, so your Factor 2 is also a dichotomy: pro versus anti. Finally, existing research of abortion attitudes suggests that gender might be an important factor, so you decide that it will be part of your design. Factor 3 is also a dichotomy: male versus female. Suddenly, we have a three-factor experiment. Let's consider a *full factorial model* first.

Full Factorial Models

A full factorial model means that all possible combinations of design factors are present in the study. We already have examined a two-factor model in the stooges study. Because both of the factors were dichotomies, the resulting study had a 2×2 or four-cell design. Now consider a three-factor model for the proposed abortion experiment. The design is shown in Exhibit 7.1. There are $2 \times 2 \times 2 = 8$ cells in the design table: one for each combination of factors. For a "balanced design," you will need the same number of subjects in each cell. Suppose you decide that $N = 5$. That means a total of 40 subjects.

Note that only the first factor, video, allows random assignment. The other factors constitute *blocking* factors. It is important to recognize a logical difference here in your ability to deduce causality. You will manipulate the video stimulus, so you should be able to make causal statements if that manipulation proves effective: Manipulate X and see what happens to Y in a context that controls other variables. You did not manipulate either gender or initial attitude. You might be able to demonstrate a relationship between gender or initial attitude and the dependent variable of subject reaction, but you could not conclude that either factor *caused* differences in reac-

Exhibit 7.1

Abortion Attitude Experiment: Full Factorial Model (*Ns*)

	Pro-Abortion Video		Anti-Abortion Video	
	Male	*Female*	*Male*	*Female*
Pro	5	5	5	5
Anti	5	5	5	5

tion. Gender represents a huge variety of variables, from genetic to social, and it correlates with many other variables. Just what caused the difference in reaction no doubt is connected with gender in some way, but the situation does not allow definitive causal statements.

An ANOVA for this experiment would have three main effects: video, gender, and initial attitude. There are also three two-way interactions possible: Video × Gender, Video × Initial Attitude, and Gender × Initial Attitude. Finally, there is one three-way interaction involving all factors simultaneously. It would be necessary, therefore, to calculate nine sums of squares, these seven plus the total and error sums of squares, and the seven matching degrees of freedom. Because the design is balanced, the only possible difficulty in interpreting results arises if any of the interactions should prove significant.

Ignore the dependent variable for a moment and think about a 2 × 2 frequency table for any pair of the factors. The Video × Gender table, for example, would have 10 cases in each cell, as would each of the other two possible tables. If you calculate any measure of association for such a table, it will equal zero. That is, because the design is full and balanced, all of the factors are statistically independent of each other; they are automatically orthogonal. Consequently, it is statistically possible to sort out the sums of squares for the different effects and proceed with ANOVA as usual.

Consider, by contrast, a survey instead of an experiment, perhaps conducted in a large university class conveniently available to the experimenter. (No, that never actually happens, does it?) It is very unlikely that either gender or prior attitude would be exactly equally divided in the class, and it is even less likely that all four gender/attitude cells would have the same number of people. If you used all members of the class, the factors would be associated by virtue of the unequal *n*s. Calculations for the different sums of squares would have problems. One somewhat questionable way in which to resolve unequal *n*s has been to randomly delete cases in the larger cells until all *n*s were equal. However, that loses power by losing cases. Often in complex tables from large surveys, you will find one or two cells with very low frequencies. Although there are methods for analyzing unbalanced designs, the advantage of a balanced design is that it makes statistical inference less subject to question. Throwing out the majority of your data to equalize *n*s is not a good option.

When there is interaction due either to unequal cell sizes or to unique joint effects, then some part of explained variance may be attributable to the variation in cell frequencies or to the common variance of the factors. The total of all explained sums of squares still is $SS_T - SS_E$. Beyond that, when interaction is present, you have to decide where to allocate any common variance or else simply make a statement about the joint effects without considering the separate main effects. A strong theory might guide you in deciding what procedure to use.

Another possibility for handling unbalanced designs is to use either effect coding or orthogonal coding to represent all main effects and their products for interaction effects, and then use multiple regression. Those approaches are beyond the scope of this volume, but Edwards (1979, p. 166) provides an example using effect coding to handle an unbalanced design. The result does not look like ANOVA, but it can generate useful answers. The SPSS manual (Norusis, 1988a) also indicates that unbalanced designs pose problems for partitioning the sums of squares and notes that solutions differ according to how one wishes to allocate the common variance.

Latin Square Designs

It should be apparent that, as the number of factors in a full factorial design increases, the number of cells in the design table increases rapidly. That, in turn, requires larger and larger samples. Exhibit 7.2 shows how quickly the number of cells increases by number of factors for either dichotomous or trichotomous factors. The problem only gets worse as we use factors with more categories than the two or three shown.

Exhibit 7.2

Number of Cells in an Experimental Design as a Function of Number of Factors

Number of Factors	Dichotomous Factors	Trichotomous Factors
1	2	3
2	4	9
3	8	27
4	16	81
5	32	243

There are several types of experimental designs other than a full factorial one. If it really is necessary to have a number of factors and you cannot afford as many cases per cell as you should have, then one alternative is a Latin square design. We will not go into the calculations for a Latin square design in any detail because they are exactly what we already are used to for main effects tests. What is different is that the calculations do not check for interactions. Therefore, one critical criterion for valid use of Latin square designs is that you can reasonably assume that the factors are not interactive. A second criterion is that all of the factors have the same number of categories. Why this is the case will become evident shortly.

Suppose we have a three-factor problem, and each factor has three categories. That would not be possible with our abortion attitude example, of course, because there are only two genders even though there could be three videos and three levels of prior attitude.

For this example, assume that we want to determine how variations in an instructional medium will affect learning and retaining information about good health practices. We have a valid and reliable dependent measure, Y, of how much has been learned and retained. Our factors are (a) the age of the communicator (20s vs. 40s vs. 60s), (b) the "scare" content of the message (soothing vs. neutral vs. scary), and (c) the technical level of the information (low vs. medium vs. high).

As evident from Exhibit 7.2, if this were a full factorial model, then the overall design of the experiment would have 27 cells. Even with only a few cases per cell, that would take a lot of time and money to complete the experiment. A Latin square design for this problem creates only a single 3 × 3 square using two of the factors and then distributes categories of the third factor within that square.

Exhibit 7.3

A Latin Square Design

		Age of Communicator		
		20s	40s	60s
	Soothing	Low	Medium	High
Scare Content	Neutral	Medium	High	Low
	Scary	High	Low	Medium

If done right, each category of each factor will appear with each category of each other factor exactly once throughout the table. Exhibit 7.3 shows such a design. There are now only 9 treatments:

1. 20s, soothing, low
2. 20s, neutral, medium
3. 20s, scary, high
4. 40s, soothing, medium
5. 40s, neutral, high
6. 40s, scary, low
7. 60s, soothing, high
8. 60s, neutral, low
9. 60s, scary, medium

If you have n cases per cell (same for all cells), then the three factors are independent (at least in design terms), just as in a full factorial design. However, because we do not have all possible combinations of factor categories, there is no way to calculate the different interactions.

We still can calculate the separate category sums for each of the three categories for each of the three factors. Note, however, that the sums for the technical factor are neither row nor column sums. They have to be taken from the correct cells within the table. As usual, each treatment effect sum of squares is obtained by squaring each category total, dividing by n, adding over all categories, and subtracting the square of the grand total divided by total number of cases. The total sum of squares is also calculated in the usual manner, as are the F tests for each main effect. If the assumption of no interaction is valid, then the design has allowed proper tests of all effects with only one third as many cases as you would need in a full factorial design. For more than three factors, there are more complex versions of this design.

Using a Quantitative Factor

So far, we have focused on discrete factors, such as gender, in experimental designs. Yet, if a theory says that a quantitative factor is causally important, then it is necessary to manipulate it to get a proper test of the causal hypothesis. The discussion in Chapter 6 introduced the idea of a quantitative factor in the context of repeated measures experiments. However, such factors can be used regardless of whether each subject experiences each level of the factor.

It would be ridiculous to create, say, 100 different values of some factor X and expose a sample of subjects to each of those values. Instead, a smaller series of values of the factor can be created and used as categories of that factor. They can be equally spaced or unequally spaced, depending on the nature of the theoretical hypothesis to be examined. In testing hypotheses about how the probability of reward affects choice behavior, it might be desirable to try 0%, 25%, 50%, 75%, and 100% as different categories of reward. However, if there was reason to suspect nonlinear effects at the extremes, then values such as 0%, 5%, 10%, and 25% might be preferable.

There is no need to consider a new ANOVA procedure for such quantitative factors because we already have done the necessary calculations in Chapter 6. The main difference is that if each subject experiences only one level of the factor, then there is no within-subjects sum of squares. All other aspects, including estimating trends over values of the factor, will follow procedures already examined.

Fixed Effects Versus Random Effects

It is assumed in the logic explored so far that each category of a factor represents a fixed value and that we have observations for all values of that factor. When the factors are manipulated by the experimenter, that assumption usually is met because the experimenter sets the factor level at the desired value. However, there are instances in which only an unsystematic sample of the possible values of a factor appears and we have no values of Y associated with the rest of the factor's values. That is especially likely to be the case in survey research. The main question raised by fixed effects versus random effects concerns making valid inferences from the observed sums of squares.

For a one-way ANOVA, there is essentially no difference between fixed and random effects models in the calculations, but the random model does allow estimating the unknown variance of X based on its observed values. To do so requires assuming that X is normally distributed. For designs with more than one factor, the sums of squares for effects are calculated in the standard way, but main effect F ratios use the mean square for interaction rather than the mean square for error in their denominators. (For further discussion of this approach and the calculation of estimates of variance for the factors, see Iversen & Norpoth, 1987.)

Split-Plot Designs

An interesting and useful category of experimental design for which ANOVA can be adapted is the split-plot design. Going back to the abortion attitude example, we can assume that the main focus of the experiment was the effect of the video stimuli. The gender and prior attitude factors are blocking factors rather than manipulated ones. They will help minimize error variance, but they are not the primary focus of the theory.

Suppose we were concerned that there may be considerable variation from subject to subject and would like to consider a repeated measures design such that each subject witnesses both videos. Is that a problem? No, the resulting design puts a repeated measures component into an otherwise factorial structure. For convenience, assume that we used only gender as the blocking factor so that each woman experiences both videos, as does each man. The order of presentation of the videos would be randomized.

Sums of squares can be calculated in such a design in the usual way. They include SS_T, SS_{Subj} that was discussed for repeated measures designs, SS_{Gender}, SS_{Video}, and SS_{Int}. It is then possible to partition SS_{Subj} into the effect of gender and random error within gender categories. $SS_{E,Gender} = SS_{Subj} - SS_{Gender}$. With their appropriate degrees of freedom, SS_{Gender} and $SS_{E,Gender}$ form an F test of the null hypothesis concerning gender. A different sum of squares can be obtained by subtraction: $SS_{Subj,Int} = SS_T - SS_{Subj} - SS_{Video} - SS_{Int}$, which, when divided by its degrees of freedom, is appropriate as the denominator of F for testing hypotheses about both the video effects and the interaction effects between gender and video. Edwards (1979, chap. 11) illustrates the procedure.

Analysis of Covariance

Although the topic requires more space than is available in this volume, the analysis of covariance, or ANCOVA, adds yet another dimension to how one can design experiments. In the original stooge study, we did not obtain prior measures of the ability of the subjects in a game like 20 Questions. However, it might be reasonable to assume that better players would evaluate the stooge's performance less highly than would poorer players, using themselves as the standard for what is a good performance. If so, then prior ability would predict some of the variation in evaluations that was treated as error in ANOVA. How could we take such variables into account without having to sort out good versus poor players in a more complex experimental design?

ANCOVA is a logical extension of ANOVA. It allows controlling the effects of continuous-level variables by statistical adjustment rather than having to use them as factors in the experimental design. The details of the procedure require understanding statistical regression, but the idea is simple enough. If better players are lower evaluators, for example, then ability and evaluation will be negatively correlated in the population and, one would expect, in the sample as well.

Regression methods allow adjusting each actual evaluation by the amount that it should be dependent on prior ability. The adjusted score represents evaluations net of the effect of ability. They will show less variance than the original evaluations did without in principle removing the variance due to the treatments (stooge roles). Therefore, ANOVA on these adjusted data will show a smaller error sum of squares but a relatively unchanged effect sum of squares. The consequence is increased effect sizes, hence greater confidence and power for the same sample size.

The essence of ANCOVA, then, is to adjust for continuous variables that are not formally a part of the experimental design. Such variables are called *covariates*. More than one covariate may be taken into account, and there are proper F tests for whether each has an effect on the dependent variable and whether each interacts with the design factors or the other covariates. (For more information about ANCOVA, see Wildt & Ahtola, 1978. For extensive treatment of regression methods, including their application to ANOVA and ANCOVA, see Pedhazur, 1982.)

Multiple Dependent Variables

One final idea about experimental design follows here. When we were considering the abortion video experiment, three possible dependent variables were suggested: attentiveness, approval, and anger. If you have multiple dependent variables, it is not necessary to run separate ANOVAs for each one. In fact, you may want to know whether all of them work together and are influenced as a set by the experimental factors.

It is too complicated to treat here, but multiple analysis of variance, or MANOVA, allows treating a set of dependent variables simultaneously. We used the SPSS MANOVA earlier to analyze the repeated measures data. Basically, MANOVA is like a complicated version of multiple regression. It creates one or more functions that describe the set of dependent variables and one or more functions that describe the set of independent variables, and it does so in a way that maximizes the extent to which the one set "explains" the other.

The main point in mentioning MANOVA here is that there are many kinds of statistical models that can accommodate complex experimental designs. Just because they are not all listed here does not mean they do not exist. It is hoped that this discussion has provided some answers, but primarily it should have prompted you to go looking for more. There is a lot out there.

Issues of Sampling and Statistical Power

The only reason to do statistical analyses, except for satisfying course requirements, is to determine to what extent and in what manner research data advance our knowledge about a substantive area. The crux of the problem lies in the fact that we almost never do research on entire populations. The obvious reasons have to do with time and money. For some research, there also are ethical problems of submitting more than the necessary number of cases to some form of experimental manipulation, such as studying the effects of new drugs that could generate harmful complications.

Representing the Population

Whenever we deal with samples, we cannot be certain that the sample will represent the population. Random sampling cannot guarantee representativeness, although some discussions of elementary statistics give that impression. All that the best sampling techniques can do is reduce the chance of nonrepresentativeness and guarantee the applicability of inferential procedures.

How can sampling methodology reduce the chance of getting an unrepresentative sample? First, the notion of randomness simply means that each case in the population has an equal chance of inclusion in the sample. For reasons we need not consider here, large sample procedures often vary the probabilities of inclusion and then use those different probabilities to weight sample evidence before using it to represent the population. For now, however, let's stick with the simple notion of equal chance.

A *simple* random sample means that any set of cases in the population can make up the sample. Simple random samples are easiest to think about but are the least efficient statistically. Suppose we select a simple random sample of 4 people from a class containing 25 women and 25 men. All we do is give each class member an equal chance of being chosen, like drawing names out of a hat, but we impose no further constraints. What is the chance that 0, 1, 2, 3, or all 4 of those people will be women?

We could readily do the calculations, but the answers are not important here. What is important is that all five possible results will have nonzero probability. Every possible gender composition could occur in our sample. The character of the sample can vary widely with a simple random sample. If we base our ideas about the population on the sample evidence, then, we have a good chance of getting misled about the gender distribution in the population.

Now consider a *stratified* sample. We will specifically choose 2 men and 2 women, perhaps by drawing women's names from one hat and men's from another. If there are equal numbers of men and women in the population, and if we select equal numbers of men and women into the sample (2, in this case), we will have maintained equal chance of inclusion for every person. The sample still will be random. However, we now have only one possible gender composition: 2 men and 2 women. Four other possible types of samples have been eliminated by stratifying, and all four would have been unrepresentative of the population in terms of gender. By eliminating a large number of possibly biased samples, we will be able to draw a smaller sample with the same confidence in our results. That is, stratified samples are more *efficient* than simple random samples.

It is important to realize, however, that stratifying increases efficiency only if the stratifying variable(s) and the dependent variable(s) are correlated. Sample representativeness is relevant only regarding the dependent variable(s) under study. We typically do not care whether our sample is unrepresentative regarding, for example, physiology or place of residence or other theoretically irrelevant dimensions. Stratifying on uncorrelated dimensions is simply a waste of time and effort. We often will not know the extent of correlation between a potential stratifying variable and a dependent variable for the particular population under study, but here again is where good theory can guide the research design.

For experimental research, we can use stratified sampling in either of two ways. First, we could designate the stratifying variable as a factor in the experiment. In that way, it becomes a *blocking* variable. Blocking simply generates parallel experiments for each stratum (e.g., for men vs. for women). This would allow explicit statistical examination of the contribution of the stratifying variable to the process under study, but it also would require larger samples. The example of gender, initial attitude, and video stimulus as factors in an experiment regarding reaction to abortion messages implies two blocking factors (gender and initial attitude), with one manipulatable design factor (video). Essentially, there will be a 2×2 table of blocking factors with manipulation of a single factor within each cell of that table. As noted previously, the sums of squares are calculated the same, but causal inference should be restricted to the manipulated factors.

Alternatively, we could simply select a stratified sample from the designated population, randomly assign cases to treatments, and proceed. The stratifying would guarantee greater representativeness, but the stratifying variable would not be incorporated formally into the statistical analysis.

Sampling methodology, especially for large surveys, can be much more complex than stratifying on a single variable. What is important for surveys or experiments is that good sample design reduces threats to external validity by reducing the chance of getting weird samples. Experimentalists often neglect sampling, as if it is enough simply to have internal validity by using good experimental methods.

Aside from questions of efficiency, there is another problem with poor sampling methods. As implied in the discussion of scope conditions (chapter 2), the results of any study speak only to the population from which the sample was drawn. If we study only college undergraduates in the laboratory, can we infer statistically beyond the population from which they were drawn? The answer is *no* unless we have a strong basis for asserting that, with reference to the subject under study, college undergraduates constitute a representative sample of the population at large.

This comment is not to denigrate a great deal of valid experimental work that has capitalized on student samples; rather, it is to get you to question carefully the appropriateness of your sample for representing the population that your theory is intended to address. Studies of real families show that age and family role both influence behavior in ways not predictable from nonfamily behavior (Leik, 1965b). Groups from real corporations, intact military units, or other established social structures carry status expectations into interaction, influencing behaviors in very specific ways (Wagner & Berger, 1993).

Without those preexisting circumstances represented in the sample, we cannot know to what extent our results can be generalized. Recently, medical researchers have begun to realize that much of what has been considered unequivocal medical fact has been derived almost exclusively from male patients or experimental subjects. What has been assumed to be general medical fact may not be so general after all.

We need to be explicit about what scope the theory is intended to have and then be sure that our sample represents the population specified in the scope conditions. Especially if we are working in a relatively new area, we would do best to start with a relatively narrow scope and carefully develop the theory as we test and revise it within that scope. Once the more restricted formulation is well established, the next phase is to begin broadening scope, gradually expanding the boundaries of the populations or circumstances we wish to address. In this sense, any given study becomes part of an integrated research program such as that described by Berger and Zelditch (1993). By being explicit about scope conditions, you are reminding yourself of the necessary conditions your sample must satisfy, and this in turn makes generalization within those conditions more appropriate.

Sample Size and Sufficient Statistical Power

There are four closely interrelated concepts having to do with how assured we can be that statistical inferences provide accurate descriptions of the populations under study. All relate to sample size. Three of these concepts were introduced earlier: significance, confidence, and effect size. The fourth is statistical power.

Remember that statistical significance concerns the chance we have of making a Type I error, that is, of incorrectly rejecting a true hypothesis. If we use formal hypothesis testing procedures, then we set our significance level, α, in advance of examining the data. Statistical confidence refers to the complement of significance. It is the probability that we are correct in rejecting a false hypothesis. Confidence, therefore, equals $1 - \alpha$. Effect size, f, is the proportion of total variance that is due to a particular explanatory factor. It should be obvious that stronger effects generate larger probabilities that we will be correct in rejecting a null hypothesis; hence effect size and confidence increase together, other things being equal. By the way, do not be confused by using f for effect size instead of F for the statistical distribution. Perhaps we could come up with a more convenient symbol for effect size, but it is helpful to retain Cohen's usage.

Power, on the other hand, refers to the chance that we will be right when we do *not* reject a hypothesis. As you recall, β is used to represent the probability of making a Type II error (incorrectly accepting a false hypothesis). Then, $1 - \beta$ is the chance that we will be correct in accepting a hypothesis. In general, as we decrease α, we increase β for any given data set, and this means that confidence and power tend to work opposite each other. However, both confidence and power are based on comparing observed systematic (i.e., explained) variances to random (i.e., unexplained) variances. We can *increase* the explained variance by increasing the accuracy of our theory and the precision with which we represent the theory in our research. We can *decrease* unexplained variance by several methods, many of which have been discussed in this book. By careful design, then, we can manage to decrease the probability of both types of errors for the same sample size. That means we can increase both confidence and power.

How can we design an experiment so that cell sizes (*ns*) will be large enough to ensure both confidence and power? Typically, experimenters or survey researchers have focused on significance, specifying just α without explicit concern for power, or $1 - \beta$. Figuring out how many cases you need in each cell of a balanced design requires specifying desired levels of both confidence and power, but you usually will find that adequate power requires greater cell size than does adequate confidence. Let's consider satisfying desired confidence first and then turn to power subsequently.

First set α, say $\alpha = .05$. That should not be arbitrary, by the way. If you are entering relatively unchartered waters, be willing to set α higher in the spirit of inquiry. If you are testing well-studied principles, then be more cautious and set α lower. Having established α, consider what effect size you would want to be able to distinguish. Remember from the earlier discussion that Cohen (1988) recommends calling an effect size of .10 low, one of .25 moderate, and one of .50 high. These are arbitrary figures, but then so are the conventional significance levels of .05 and .01. Remember that the effect size is the ratio of the particular effect sum of squares to the error sum of squares.

It is hard to consider what effect size is substantively or theoretically important if you have not done research in a particular area before, but one reasonable strategy would be to check carefully the ANOVA tables of any prior research reports that deal with the factors and/or dependent variables you want to study. If there is much prior work in the literature, then you should be able to get a sense of what effect sizes have been observed previously, even though they often are not reported, and judge from that how big an effect size would help further the collective research enterprise. It is quite possible that you would choose different effect sizes for different main effects.

For convenience, let's say you chose a moderate effect size of .25. Your α of .05 means you want to be at least 95% confident in rejecting a null hypothesis if such an effect is present. The critical value of F

from the F table is related to the sums of squares, number of cells, number of categories, and cell size as follows:

$$F = \frac{SS_{effect}/df_{effect}}{SS_E/df_E}$$

$$= \frac{SS_{effect}}{SS_E} \frac{df_E}{df_{effect}}$$

$$= f \frac{(n-1)c}{J-1}$$

so that

$$n = 1 + \frac{(J-1)F}{fc}$$

where

f is the desired effect size,

c is the total number of cells in the table,

J is the number of categories in the factor being tested, and

n is the number of cases per cell.

Let's consider again our hypothetical study of reactions to messages about abortion. There are three dichotomies generating an eight-cell design, so $c = 8$. Each main effect is a dichotomy, meaning $J = 2$ for all factors. With a desired effect size of .25, then, the preceding equation says that $n = 1 + F/2$ because $J - 1 = 1$ and $cf = (8)(.25) = 2$. Now we enter an iterative process, as shown in Exhibit 7.4. Try a cell size, check the F table, enter the critical value of F into the equation, and see whether you get the same n back. If necessary, revise n until the process works. Suppose we try 5 cases per cell. Consulting the F table, we find no row for denominator $df = (8)(5 - 1) = 32$. To be conservative, use $df = 30$. For $\alpha = .05$ and dfs of 1 and 30, $F = 2.09$. Returning to the equation, we find that $n = 1 + 4.18/2$, or approximately 3. This clearly is not the 5 we started with, so let's use the 3 and try again. This time we have denominator f of $(8)(3 - 1) = 16$ and a table F of 4.49. Again solving the equation gives a new n of 3.25. Although this is close, using only 3 cases per cell would give slightly less than the desired confidence. Therefore, an n of 4 should be chosen to satisfy the confidence criterion.

Exhibit 7.4

Setting Cell Size to Ensure Desired Confidence

1. Set a trial value of n.

2. Find the critical value of F for that n with $df = J - 1, c(n - 1)$.

3. Enter the critical value of F in the equation and calculate n based on that F.

4. If calculated n equals trial n, then you are done; if not, then set trial n at the calculated value and start over.

Now what about power? It will be necessary to consult tables such as those provided by Cohen (1988) to solve this aspect of our sample size question. If we keep the same f of .25, α of .05, and numerator df of 1, then we can consult his tables for setting ANOVA sample sizes. There we find that we would need a total sample size (all cells included) of 85 to attain power = .90. That implies 10.63 cases per cell, rounded to $n = 11$. For power equal to our confidence level of .95, Cohen's table indicates that we would need 105 total cases, or 13.25 per cell. We could round down to $n = 13$ for a very slight drop in power or increase to 14 for a slight increase in power. In either case, note that the power criterion for sample size generated a larger n than did the confidence criterion.

Keep in mind that both confidence and power rely on our assumed effect size. If the actual effect size is markedly lower than we had assumed, then both power and confidence will diminish. On the other hand, greater effect size than anticipated would mean you would have greater power and confidence than anticipated. Finding after the experiment is over that effect size was well below that assumed when the design was being worked out is both frustrating and embarrassing because we find that we simply cannot make inferences with the confidence and power we wanted.

Remember that power refers to our being assured that *no* effect of size f or larger is present in the population when we *cannot* reject a null hypothesis. Because not rejecting the null hypothesis should be just as important theoretically as rejecting it, we do not want to be wishy-washy about failure to reject. Ideally, α and β should be equal. There is an unfortunate bias in most scientific work that treats positive findings (rejecting a null hypothesis) as more important than negative findings (not rejecting). That bias implies that we fail to recognize that ruling out possible explanations is just as important in furthering knowledge as is finding some new possible explanation.

Returning to the example, the 4 cases per cell that we calculated to ensure adequate confidence looks a bit anemic in terms of power. Even $n = 5$ will generate power of only about .60. If time, money, and/or other factors prohibit as many as 11 cases per cell, then there are three options. One is to be satisfied with lower power and interpret null results very cautiously. Failure to reject a null hypothesis might mean only that we just do not have enough power to be sure that an effect is not present in the population.

A second option is to alter the effect level we wish to distinguish. For an effect size of $f = .50$, we could have power = .90 with just 22 cases, or 3 per cell. That means, however, that if we cannot reject the null hypothesis, then the best we can say is that there is a 90% chance that there is no large effect in the population. Such a statement says nothing about whether a smaller effect is present.

A third option is to set α higher so that β can be lower and power can be higher for the same sample size. For $\alpha = .10$ with $f = .25$, we would need 69 cases total, or 9 cases per cell, to achieve $\beta = .10$. That is a savings of almost one third of the cases compared to when α and $\beta = .05$.

If we really want to do the job right, then we had better plan for a sufficient number of cases, and this means to budget both time and finances accordingly. As commented earlier, the power criterion required a larger sample than did the significance criterion. It usually will be more efficient to determine n for desired power first and then check to see whether it satisfies desired significance requirements as well.

Testing What We Really Believe

There is a danger in the way in which statistical methods are taught. That danger lies in endless repetition of the notion of a null hypothesis that we do not really believe versus a substantive hypothesis that we do believe. Of course, statistical tests are set up in null form, and there is no way to avoid that. The difficulty is that *null* usually is interpreted as a total absence of systematic pattern in the data. Theories, on the other hand, predict specific patterns. How can we test theories adequately with tests that deny what the theory predicts?

Revisiting the Null Hypothesis

Let us go briefly over the logic behind a one-way ANOVA once again to have a basis for departing from the usual approach. The within sum of squares concerns variation of observed values around group-specific predicted values, and the between sum of squares concerns variation between those group-specific predicted values. Each constitutes a numerator of an estimate of population variance. If there are no group differences in the population, then any observed group differences should be the result of random variation, and that random variation should be a function of the overall variation in the population.

The F distribution specifies the chance that two independent estimates of the same population variance will disagree by any given amount. The F test, then, is simply a comparison of two estimates of what will be the same variance if the groups do not differ in the population. Rejecting the underlying premise of "if the groups do not differ" means accepting the contrary: "The groups do differ."

For the usual null form of the test, the values predicted for each group are the group means, whatever they turn out to be. The null hypothesis becomes "The group means do not differ in the population," and the alternative to that null hypothesis is "Oh, yes they do." Notice that there is no room here for specific predicted values. We act as if our theory is incapable of asserting anything other than that some unspecified difference is to be expected. As one example:

> Substantive: The stooge's apparent confidence will affect how others evaluate his or her objective contributions.
>
> Null: The stooge's apparent confidence will not affect how others evaluate his or her objective contributions.

As another example:

> Substantive: Pro-abortionists will respond differently from anti-abortionists to video stimuli about abortions.
>
> Null: Response to video stimuli about abortions will be unrelated to prior attitude about abortions.

These are very general statements. We have said nothing about what the population means might be except different versus not different. Maybe we do not know enough to be more explicit, but the more we study a given subject, the more we *should* be able to make explicit predictions.

With a clear enough theory, especially one that is expressed in mathematical or computer simulation form, we can derive explicit predictions rather than "whatever the means turn out to be" predictions. Then our tests should incorporate those explicit predictions rather than relying on explanation in the form of observed cell means. Although it takes a bit of rethinking, such an approach requires nothing new of ANOVA.

An Example of Specific Predictions

Consider the experimental work on power in social exchange networks that has been described in previous chapters. (Careful, now, this is social power we are focusing on, not statistical power.) There has been such careful and extensive work in this area that very specific mathematical models of network power have been developed and computer simulations have been written. Although the two major theoretical traditions currently differ somewhat in their formulations, each can generate very precise predictions that reflect observed data to a high degree.

The typical experiment involves successive dyadic bargaining for distribution of joint profits. If no agreement can be reached in a given cycle (exchange period), then that dyad gets no profit to divide. In the most common version, each person can take part in only one exchange per cycle. If a dyad agrees to an exchange, then 24 points are divided between them according to their prior agreement. Any subject not in an exchange on a given cycle receives nothing.

Assume a network in which A, B, and C all can bargain with each other but D can only bargain with A. A has three alternative bargaining contacts, B and C each have two, and D has only one. Further, if A, who is D's only contact, decides to deal with someone else, then D is left out in the cold. Over time, subjects come to realize that they are relatively advantaged or disadvantaged in their bargaining, and the share of profits departs fairly rapidly from 50/50 to one dependent on relative positions in the network.

The different theoretical formulations may disagree somewhat, but each predicts very precise values for what the average "take" should be in each structural position. If the data are analyzed by the usual substantive versus null hypothesis approach, then all that we can hypothesize, regardless of which theoretical approach we take, is that "The average take will differ across positions in the network." Again, all the null hypothesis can say is "No, it won't." Even if we can reject the null hypothesis, we have not validated the specific predictions of the theory. "Different" is not the same as "A will average 18 points and D will average 6 points."

The ideal test should be as precise as possible given the state of our theory, and the idea of theory should be to make as precise a statement of predictions as possible. In this light, the typical "There will be a difference" versus "There won't be any difference" is the *least informative form a theory can take*. Tests of such minimal predictions constitute the least possible furthering of our substantive knowledge. Willer (1987) provides a more extended discussion of this very important but often ignored problem with the current state of much theory and research.

Implications of Specific Tests

It is not difficult to construct an appropriate statistical test of specific predictions within the logic discussed in this book. There are two approaches, but one is by far the easiest, and so only it will be addressed. In fact, there is an example of this approach in the discussion of MANOVA in the *SPSS/PC+ Advanced Statistics* manual (Norusis, 1988b). All that is needed is to subtract the specific predictions for each condition from the observed values for that condition. Let's call these differences *corrected scores*. The within sum of squares is now random variation of the corrected scores ("errors" in terms of the model's predictions), and the various factor sums of squares now represent the extent to which the category means of the corrected scores differ across the categories of those factors.

Now, stop and think a moment. With the standard null hypothesis approach, we concluded that rejecting the null meant that we substantiated the substantive theory. But if we have subtracted a precise expected value from each observation, and if our theory is absolutely correct, then all of the corrected scores will represent pure random error. All population cell means for the corrected scores should equal *zero* if the theory is true. Any variation among cell means that exceeds random variation, based on cell sample size and the within variance, indicates that the predictions are incorrect.

This is a complete and important reversal of the usual logic. Given that we have used specific predictions to create corrected scores, our theory is validated to the extent that we *cannot* reject the null hypothesis. What does that mean about the importance of α versus β? We have discussed power quite a bit in this chapter, but with the usual substantive versus null hypothesis in mind. Now the null hypothesis *is* the substantive hypothesis. If we cannot reject it, then we substantiate our theory. But can we be confident in our failure to reject?

That is what β and power are all about. If we can move to more precise formulations of theory and more appropriate tests via creating corrected scores as deviations of observations from predictions, then we absolutely must be concerned with statistical power. When failure to reject constitutes evidence in support of the theory, we need to be sure that such failure is not just because power is weak (our sample is too small, our measurement is too sloppy, etc.).

There is nothing about this discussion that implies that the statistical procedures detailed in this book are wrong or need to be changed. The only implication is that we need to rethink how we make theoretical predictions and how we use methods such as ANOVA to test those predictions. Many substantive areas have specific prediction forms such as power equations for stimulus-response curves or logistic equations for epidemiological processes. Those are the predictions we should be testing, not predictions of unspecified difference.

Statistical Significance, Theoretical Importance, and Practical Utility

Our long excursion is nearly over. There is one remaining area that deserves a brief discussion. We tend to get so wrapped up in the question of statistical significance that we often ignore other questions about the importance of our findings. Toward that end, it is convenient to distinguish three different types of importance: statistical significance, theoretical importance, and practical utility.

Statistical Significance

Statistical significance pertains only to the chance that random sampling could produce results in the sample that are not present in the population. Standard significance tests are so de rigueur that we seldom think about them or even about the relevance of different values of α. Unfortunately, as commented earlier, it is harder to publish null results than it is to publish significant results, so most researchers spend their time looking for significance to justify getting into print.

Perhaps if we become more careful about statistical power, the idea of null results as contributions to knowledge will become more acceptable. Especially if we move to testing specific predictions, null results will constitute exactly what we want to publish. In any event, knowledge grows by finding both what does work and what does not work. Null results, even in the traditional tests, are important because they demonstrate that effects previously thought to be plausible are not present.

This commentary is intended not to argue against continual concern with statistical significance but rather to urge that it be considered as only one criterion in deciding how results should be interpreted and evaluating their contribution to knowledge. As is well known, if a sample is large enough, everything becomes statistically significant. That is, the smallest departure from expectation can reject a null hypothesis if we have a few million cases. Similarly, with very small samples, even the most startling effects can disappear under the harsh glare of the significance test.

In short, be an intelligent user of significance testing. You want to be reasonably confident that your results are not flukes of happenstance, but you do not want to throw out interesting leads or bury important findings of no difference just because of a predilection to say "If it isn't significant, forget it."

Theoretical Importance

The question of how important a finding is for a theory has nothing to do with sampling happenstance. Therefore, it is entirely separate from statistical significance. Theoretical importance concerns the extent to which knowledge is advanced. More precisely, the theoretical importance of any research finding is the extent to which it enhances our ability to understand, explain, and predict in the substantive area of interest.

To a considerable extent, the really important advances in theory come from ideas rather than from data. The data test the ideas, of course, and a continual interplay of ideas and evidence ensures that our substantive theories do not wander off into the nebulous realms of pure imagination. Particular substantive findings can be theoretically important in two ways.

The most obvious is the direct check on whether crucial propositions or formulations hold up in the light of objective reality. The more central the proposition or formulation is to the overall theory, the more important the empirical test is for that theory. A tree analogy might be appropriate here. An extensive theory often will have some basic principles on which everything else depends. If those principles are found invalid, the tree loses its trunk and the entire theory crashes. On the other hand, invalidating a minor branch on the theory tree need not threaten the trunk or even the other branches.

As noted previously, null findings are just as important in this regard as are findings that substantiate predictions. Discovering evidence that a basic postulate does not hold raises serious questions about either the theory in general or the scope conditions that specify the range of applicability of that theory. There is a tendency to get attached to theories, especially if one has published work based on them, such that scholars often ignore negative evidence and go right on asserting the same ideas. Several historical examples can easily be cited of theories that lasted in the literature for years after extensive evidence had demonstrated their inability to explain or predict.

Whenever an empirical test focuses on a trunk of a theoretical structure, it is necessary to be very careful about confidence and power. Suppose someone were to challenge the foundations of relativity theory. Would it make sense to do so with, say, α and β in the .50 range? Of course not. The theoretical importance of the work would be too great to have a 50/50 chance of reaching the wrong conclusions.

On the other hand, when only a minor theoretical branch that looks interesting is involved in a test, there is no reason to be terribly concerned with either α or β. What ought to count is the possibility of some new leads or intriguing hints leading to a better way of thinking about and explaining what we are interested in. A considerable effect size, even with small samples, suggests something worth further examination. This is the second way in which empirical work can be theoretically important: It can generate new ideas.

For all the attempted rigor and precision in any scientific field, there is some sense of serendipity behind just about every major advance. We hear or read about dramatic breakthroughs in science but seldom about merely significant results. The drama is less in the data than it is in the ideas—in the way of formulating or expressing the problem.

Good theory is at least part art; it cannot thrive in a desert of nothing but formal criteria even though formalization can greatly enhance the understanding and application of the intuitive. Part of the research enterprise should be to allow interesting anomalies and puzzling departures to be observed and explored. The deviant case may be just as theoretically important as the demonstration of overall coherence and predictability.

Practical Utility

The last topic listed at the outset of this chapter was practical utility. Scholars are likely to differ widely on the relevance of practical matters for questions of theory and research. For some, *practical* or *applied* is thought of as of lesser stature. To others, unless research has practical utility, it is a waste of time and effort. This is not the place for such a debate, but it is relevant to distinguish practical utility from the other types of importance.

The practical utility of a theory or body of knowledge is the extent to which it enables prediction of and control over aspects of the real world. Every government is faced constantly with a need for useful knowledge. What will next year's employment situation be? How will that affect the tax base? Similarly, industry needs practical answers about effective methods, costs, and sales potential. If we change our logo, will we gain or lose customers? How much are profits likely to increase if we spend these millions on changing our product line? All these are very practical problems. None of them can be answered adequately without empirically verified theories.

Some very elegant and valid theories may be of little practical utility, whereas other less well-formulated and -tested theories may nevertheless have considerable practical use. It is common in social sciences, for example, to use as explanatory variables a range of factors that are not subject to manipulation: age, race, gender, social status, and so forth. No matter how powerful any of those factors is in statistical terms, and no matter how central (and thus important) such a factor might be in theoretical terms, it has little practical utility because it is not directly subject to policy controls. The extensive legislative efforts regarding equal opportunity and their often discouraging impacts, for example, demonstrate the necessity to find manipulatable factors rather than simply saying that race and/or gender matter. Similarly, suppose that a theory of educational aspiration is couched totally in terms of race, class, and gender. Then that theory says absolutely nothing about how educational policy might be changed so as to enhance the aspirations of future students. The nonmanipulatable factors might explain why things are or are not working, but only manipulatable variables are useful for revising policy toward accomplishing some end.

In short, practical utility may be quite different from either statistical significance or theoretical importance. That is why many people in both business and government become impatient with the usual university model of theory and research. Too often, there is a lack of understanding that explanation does not necessarily lead to the ability to generate desired effects.

Of Theory and Statistics

Not all research needs or should even attempt to satisfy the criteria of significance, importance, and utility. The most effective model involves research programs that cover the range from very detailed, controlled experimental tests of small pieces of an overall puzzle to broad attempts to assess the utility of knowledge by trying to apply it to real-world problems. It is unlikely that a single theory will cover that full range.

The history of statistical inference is one of looking for ways in which to make reasonable conclusions about empirical data. When a problem comes up in research for which there is no appropriate statistical model, either of two paths can be taken. A common but undesirable path is to say "Oh, well, I guess I can't do this project then." That would result in passing up the chance to do something interesting. The better route would be to tell the statisticians "Look here, we need something new."

The point is that statistical methodology never should drive theory, nor should it determine research. That would be like letting the tools in your workshop determine what you are going to build. Practical problems always arise and need verifiable knowledge for adequate solutions. General theoretical problems always arise and need new ideas and insights to allow further progress. We should collectively push for more accurate theories and models, more precise testing of exactly what our theories and models predict, and more useful results. The statistical models discussed in this book can help with those goals, but if you encounter problems for which they are not suited, do not be deterred. Just find some new tools and push ahead. There are lots of other methods out there.

Appendix
The **F** *Distribution*

The F Distribution

The top value in each row is the necessary F value to reject the hypothesis at $\alpha = 0.05$. The second value is for $\alpha = 0.01$.

df	1	2	3	4	5	6	7	8	9	10	20	50	1000
						Numerator degrees of freedom							
1	161.45	199.50	215.71	224.58	230.16	233.99	236.77	238.88	240.54	241.88	248.01	251.77	254.19
	4052.18	4999.50	5403.35	5624.58	5763.65	5858.99	5928.36	5981.07	6022.47	6055.85	6208.73	6302.52	6362.68
2	18.51	19.00	19.16	19.25	19.30	19.33	19.35	19.37	19.38	19.40	19.45	19.48	19.49
	98.50	99.00	99.17	99.25	99.30	99.33	99.36	99.37	99.39	99.40	99.45	99.48	99.50
3	10.13	9.55	9.28	9.12	9.01	8.94	8.89	8.85	8.81	8.79	8.66	8.58	8.53
	34.12	30.82	29.46	28.71	28.24	27.91	27.67	27.49	27.35	27.23	26.69	26.35	26.14
4	7.71	6.94	6.59	6.39	6.26	6.16	6.09	6.04	6.00	5.96	5.80	5.70	5.63
	21.20	18.00	16.69	15.98	15.52	15.21	14.98	14.80	14.66	14.55	14.02	13.69	13.47
5	6.61	5.79	5.41	5.19	5.05	4.95	4.88	4.82	4.77	4.74	4.56	4.44	4.37
	16.26	13.27	12.06	11.39	10.97	10.67	10.46	10.29	10.16	10.05	9.55	9.24	9.03
6	5.99	5.14	4.76	4.53	4.39	4.28	4.21	4.15	4.10	4.06	3.87	3.75	3.67
	13.75	10.92	9.78	9.15	8.75	8.47	8.26	8.10	7.98	7.87	7.40	7.09	6.89
7	5.59	4.74	4.35	4.12	3.97	3.87	3.79	3.73	3.68	3.64	3.44	3.32	3.23
	12.25	9.55	8.45	7.85	7.46	7.19	6.99	6.84	6.72	6.62	6.16	5.86	5.66
8	5.32	4.46	4.07	3.84	3.69	3.58	3.50	3.44	3.39	3.35	3.15	3.02	2.93
	11.26	8.65	7.59	7.01	6.63	6.37	6.18	6.03	5.91	5.81	5.36	5.07	4.87
9	5.12	4.26	3.86	3.63	3.48	3.37	3.29	3.23	3.18	3.14	2.94	2.80	2.71
	10.56	8.02	6.99	6.42	6.06	5.80	5.61	5.47	5.35	5.26	4.81	4.52	4.32
10	4.96	4.10	3.71	3.48	3.33	3.22	3.14	3.07	3.02	2.98	2.77	2.64	2.54
	10.04	7.56	6.55	5.99	5.64	5.39	5.20	5.06	4.94	4.85	4.41	4.12	3.92
11	4.84	3.98	3.59	3.36	3.20	3.09	3.01	2.95	2.90	2.85	2.65	2.51	2.41
	9.65	7.21	6.22	5.67	5.32	5.07	4.89	4.74	4.63	4.54	4.10	3.81	3.61
12	4.75	3.89	3.49	3.26	3.11	3.00	2.91	2.85	2.80	2.75	2.54	2.40	2.30
	9.33	6.93	5.95	5.41	5.06	4.82	4.64	4.50	4.39	4.30	3.86	3.57	3.37
13	4.67	3.81	3.41	3.18	3.03	2.92	2.83	2.77	2.71	2.67	2.46	2.31	2.21
	9.07	6.70	5.74	5.21	4.86	4.62	4.44	4.30	4.19	4.10	3.66	3.38	3.18
14	4.60	3.74	3.34	3.11	2.96	2.85	2.76	2.70	2.65	2.60	2.39	2.24	2.14
	8.86	6.51	5.56	5.04	4.69	4.46	4.28	4.14	4.03	3.94	3.51	3.22	3.02

df	1	2	3	4	5	Numerator degrees of freedom 6	7	8	9	10	20	50	1000
15	4.54	3.68	3.29	3.06	2.90	2.79	2.71	2.64	2.59	2.54	2.33	2.18	2.07
	8.68	6.36	5.42	4.89	4.56	4.32	4.14	4.00	3.89	3.80	3.37	3.08	2.88
16	4.49	3.63	3.24	3.01	2.85	2.74	2.66	2.59	2.54	2.49	2.28	2.12	2.02
	8.53	6.23	5.29	4.77	4.44	4.20	4.03	3.89	3.78	3.69	3.26	2.97	2.76
17	4.45	3.59	3.20	2.96	2.81	2.70	2.61	2.55	2.49	2.45	2.23	2.08	1.97
	8.40	6.11	5.18	4.67	4.34	4.10	3.93	3.79	3.68	3.59	3.16	2.87	2.66
18	4.41	3.55	3.16	2.93	2.77	2.66	2.58	2.51	2.46	2.41	2.19	2.04	1.92
	8.29	6.01	5.09	4.58	4.25	4.01	3.84	3.71	3.60	3.51	3.08	2.78	2.58
19	4.38	3.52	3.13	2.90	2.74	2.63	2.54	2.48	2.42	2.38	2.16	2.00	1.88
	8.18	5.93	5.01	4.50	4.17	3.94	3.77	3.63	3.52	3.43	3.00	2.71	2.50
20	4.35	3.49	3.10	2.87	2.71	2.60	2.51	2.45	2.39	2.35	2.12	1.97	1.85
	8.10	5.85	4.94	4.43	4.10	3.87	3.70	3.56	3.46	3.37	2.94	2.64	2.43
25	4.24	3.39	2.99	2.76	2.60	2.49	2.40	2.34	2.28	2.24	2.01	1.84	1.72
	7.77	5.57	4.68	4.18	3.85	3.63	3.46	3.32	3.22	3.13	2.70	2.40	2.18
30	4.17	3.32	2.92	2.69	2.53	2.42	2.33	2.27	2.21	2.16	1.93	1.76	1.63
	7.56	5.39	4.51	4.02	3.70	3.47	3.30	3.17	3.07	2.98	2.55	2.25	2.02
40	4.08	3.23	2.84	2.61	2.45	2.34	2.25	2.18	2.12	2.08	1.84	1.66	1.52
	7.31	5.18	4.31	3.83	3.51	3.29	3.12	2.99	2.89	2.80	2.37	2.06	1.82
50	4.03	3.18	2.79	2.56	2.40	2.29	2.20	2.13	2.07	2.03	1.78	1.60	1.45
	7.17	5.06	4.20	3.72	3.41	3.19	3.02	2.89	2.78	2.70	2.27	1.95	1.70
75	3.97	3.12	2.73	2.49	2.34	2.22	2.13	2.06	2.01	1.96	1.71	1.52	1.35
	6.99	4.90	4.05	3.58	3.27	3.05	2.89	2.76	2.65	2.57	2.13	1.81	1.53
100	3.94	3.09	2.70	2.46	2.31	2.19	2.10	2.03	1.97	1.93	1.68	1.48	1.30
	6.90	4.82	3.98	3.51	3.21	2.99	2.82	2.69	2.59	2.50	2.07	1.74	1.45
1000	3.85	3.00	2.61	2.38	2.22	2.11	2.02	1.95	1.89	1.84	1.58	1.36	1.11
	6.66	4.63	3.80	3.34	3.04	2.82	2.66	2.53	2.43	2.34	1.90	1.54	1.16

References

Arney, W. R. (1990). *Understanding statistics in the social sciences*. New York: W. H. Freeman.

Asch, S. E. (1951). Effects of group pressure upon the modification and distortion of judgements. In H. Guetzkow (Ed.), *Groups, leadership and men* (pp. 177-190). Pittsburgh, PA: Carnegie Press.

Babbie, E., & Halley, F. (1994). *Adventures in social research*. Thousand Oaks, CA: Pine Forge.

Berger, J., & Zelditch, M., Jr. (1993). *Theoretical research programs*. Stanford, CA: Stanford University Press.

Bion, W. R. (1959). *Experiences in groups*. New York: Basic Books.

Bunge, M. (1979). *Causality and modern science* (3rd ed.). New York: Dover.

Campbell, D. T., & Stanley, J. (1963). *Experimental and quasi-experimental designs for research*. Chicago: Rand McNally.

Cochran, W. G., & Cox, G. (1957). *Experimental design*. New York: John Wiley.

Cohen, J. (1988). *Statistical power analysis for the behavioral sciences* (2nd ed.). Hillsdale, NJ: Lawrence Erlbaum.

Collyer, C. E., & Enns, J. T. (1986). *Analysis of variance: The basic designs*. Chicago: Nelson-Hall.

Cook, K. S. (Ed.). (1987). *Social exchange theory*. Newbury Park, CA: Sage.

Cook, K., Gillmore, M. R., & Yamagishi, T. (1983). The distribution of power in exchange networks: Theory and experimental results. *American Journal of Sociology, 89*, 275-305.

Edwards, A. L. (1979). *Multiple regression and the analysis of variance and covariance*. New York: W. H. Freeman.

Estes, W. K. (1991). *Statistical models in behavioral research*. Hillsdale, NJ: Lawrence Erlbaum.

Fisher, R. A. (1935). *The design of experiments*. Edinburgh, Scotland: Oliver and Boyd. (9th ed. published in 1971)

Gaito, J. (1965). Unequal intervals and unequal n's in trend analysis. *Psychological Bulletin, 63*, 125-127.

Hage, J., & Meeker, B. F. (1988). *Social causality*. Boston: Unwin Hyman.

Hurlburt, R. T. (1994). *Comprehending behavioral statistics*. Pacific Grove, CA: Brooks/Cole.

Iversen, G. R., & Norpoth, H. (1987). *Analysis of variance* (2nd ed.). Newbury Park, CA: Sage.

Jaccard, J., & Becker, M. A. (1990). *Statistics for the behavioral sciences*. Belmont, CA: Wadsworth.

Lakatos, I. (1978). *The methodology of scientific research programmes*. Cambridge, England: Cambridge University Press.

Leik, R. K. (1965a). Irrelevant aspects of stooge behavior: Implications for leadership studies and experimental methodology. *Sociometry, 28*, 259-271.

Leik, R. K. (1965b). Type of group and the probability of initiating acts. *Sociometry, 28*, 57-65.

Leik, R. K. (1992). New directions in network exchange theory: Strategic manipulation of network linkages. *Social Networks, 14*, 309-323.

Loether, H. J., & McTavish, D. G. (1993). *Descriptive and inferential statistics: An introduction* (4th ed.). Boston: Allyn & Bacon.

Markovsky, B., Willer, D., & Patton, T. (1988). Power relations in exchange networks. *American Sociological Review, 53*, 220-236.

Meeker, B. F., & Leik, R. K. (1994). Experimentation in sociological social psychology. In K. Cook, G. Fine, & J. S. House (Eds.), *Sociological perspectives on social psychology* (pp. 629-649). Boston: Allyn & Bacon.

New World Dictionaries. (1983). *Webster's new universal unabridged dictionary* (2nd ed.). Cleveland, OH: Author.

Norusis, M. J. (1988a). *SPSS/PC+ V2.0 base manual.* Chicago: SPSS, Inc.

Norusis, M. J. (1988b). *SPSS/PC+ advanced statistics* (Vol. 2.0). Chicago: SPSS, Inc.

O'Rourke, J. F. (1963). Field and laboratory: The decision-making behavior of family groups in two experimental conditions. *Sociometry, 26*, 422-435.

Parsons, T. (1961). An outline of the social system. In T. Parsons, E. Shils, K. D. Naegele, & J. R. Pitts (Eds.), *Theories of society* (pp. 30-79). New York: Free Press.

Pedhazur, E. J. (1982). *Multiple regression in behavioral research.* New York: Holt, Rinehart & Winston.

Random House. (1991). *Random House Webster's college dictionary.* New York: Author.

Solomon, R. L. (1949). Extension of control group design. *Psychological Bulletin, 46*, 137-150.

Tuckerman, B. W., & Jensen, M. A. C. (1977). Stages in small group development revisited. *Group and Organizational Studies, 2*, 419-427.

Wagner, D. G., & Berger, J. (1993). Status characteristics theory: The growth of a program. In J. Berger & M. Zelditch, Jr. (Eds.), *Theoretical research programs* (pp. 23-63). Stanford, CA: Stanford University Press.

Weick, K. (1971). Group processes, family processes, and problem solving. In J. Aldous, T. Condon, R. Hill, M. Straus, & I. Tallman (Eds.), *Family problem solving* (pp. 3-32). Hillsdale, NJ: Dryden.

Wheelan, S. A. (1994). *Group processes: A developmental perspective.* Boston: Allyn & Bacon.

Wildt, A. R., & Ahtola, O. T. (1978). *Analysis of covariance.* Beverly Hills, CA: Sage.

Willer, D. (1987). *Theory and the experimental investigation of social structures.* New York: Gordon & Breach.

Index